The Maryland
Adventure

GIBBS SMITH EDUCATION
TO ENRICH AND INSPIRE HUMANKIND

This textbook is dedicated to the students and teachers of Maryland for their inspiration and to Jenny, Duncan, Amanda, Mike, and Suzannah.

Second Edition
© 2010 Gibbs Smith, Publisher
All rights reserved. No part of this book
may be reproduced by any means whatsoever,
either mechanical or electronic, without
permission from the publisher.

Published by
Gibbs Smith, Publisher
PO Box 667
Layton, UT 84041
801-544-9800
www.gibbs-smith.com/textbooks

Managing Editor: Aimee Stoddard
Editorial Assistants: Jennifer Petersen, Kris Brunson, Erin Flinders
Education Editors: Clarissa Coley, Natalie Richins, Nancy Bosse
Photo Editors: Wendy Knight, Janis J. Hansen
Cover and Book Design: J. Vehar
Maps and Graphs: J. Vehar

Cover Photo Credits: The Inner Harbor of Baltimore—1983
© 2008 by Paul McGehee
paulmcgeheeart.com

Printed and bound in China
ISBN-13: 978-1-4236-0583-6
ISBN-10: 1-4236-0583-7

19 18 17 16 15 14 13 12 11 10   1 2 3 4 5

ABOUT THE AUTHOR

Suzanne Ellery Chapelle earned her BA in American history at Harvard University and PhD at the Johns Hopkins University. She is professor emerita at Morgan State University. For 37 years, Dr. Chapelle taught American history courses, including the History of Maryland, the Ethnic Experience in America, Urban History, and the Environmental Crisis in Historical Perspective. Over the years, she taught many undergraduate students, who aspired to be teachers, and graduate students, who were teachers. She is the author of six books, most of which explore various aspects of Maryland history. Dr. Chapelle considers textbooks to be one way to open children's eyes to the world around them and to let them share in the experiences of many different people.

Contents

Maps

What Do You Think?

Linking the Present to the Past

Maryland Portraits

Special Pages

Chapter Review

Skills Activities

Go to the Source

Reference

Begin the Adventure

What's the Big Idea?

Historians use tools to learn about the past.

Southern troops guarded Antietam Bridge during the Civil War. You will read about this war later in your study of our state's history. **What material was this bridge made out of?**

Chapter 1

Are you ready to start a great adventure? Your journey through Maryland history is one of the most fantastic adventures you could take. You will get to learn about many different places in Maryland, exciting events from our state's past, and Maryland people who accomplished amazing things.

Before you set off on your adventure, you will first learn about tools that will help you along the way. Your textbook will be the main tool you use on your adventure through Maryland history. You will also learn about the tools people use to study history.

KEY IDEA

The Maryland Adventure is one tool you can use to learn about the history of Maryland.

WORDS TO UNDERSTAND

caption
century
decade
glossary
index
itinerary
portrait
table of contents
timeline

It is necessary to take tools on every adventure. **What tools are shown on this page?**

Discovering Your Tools

Welcome to *The Maryland Adventure*. Learning about Maryland is like going on a great adventure. Have you ever been on one? Maybe you have gone rafting on white-water rapids. You might have tried hiking or rock climbing. What kinds of tools did you need on your adventure? Did you take a flashlight, a life jacket, or ropes? As you study Maryland history, you will use some important tools to help you along the way. Your textbook is one tool. Let's take a closer look at how your textbook is a tool.

4

Primary Sources

Primary sources are firsthand accounts or original objects from the past. Primary sources were made, used, or written by people who were involved in an event or who saw it happen. Studying things people made, used, or wrote long ago tells us a lot about their lives.

Artifacts

Artifacts are important primary sources. **Artifacts** are objects people made or used in the past and then left behind. A handmade Indian basket is one example of an artifact. By studying it, you might be able to tell how people made it and what materials they used to make it. You might also learn something about the person's life.

An old trunk and a black-and-white picture are primary sources. **Why are they primary sources?**

Photographs

Photographs are also primary sources. Photos record how people looked and dressed. Photos might also record events that took place. Studying photographs from the past can help you gather information about a certain place or time.

Newspapers and Magazines

Newspapers and magazines from the past can also be primary sources. They recorded important events when they happened. They told stories of people who saw, or **witnessed**, an event. Studying newspapers or magazines from the past tells us more about people and events.

Newspapers are primary sources because they record current events. **Why do you think newspapers are printed on large sheets of thin paper?**

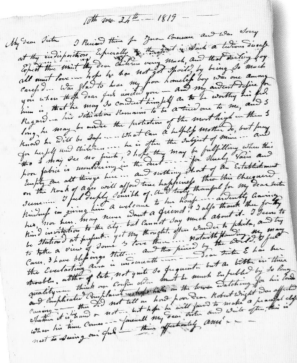

Journals and Letters

Papers, letters, journals, and other *documents* can be primary sources, too. They tell about people, places, and events from the past. Some of them tell us how people felt and what their lives were like.

Oral History

Oral history is spoken history that one person tells to another. Sometimes this type of history is later written down. Other times it is saved as an audio or video recording. Can you guess why historians love to study oral histories?

A letter is a primary source because it was written by someone who lived at a particular time. **In what year was this letter written?**

Recognize Primary and Secondary Sources

On a piece of paper, draw a chart like the one below. Then, look through the book to find one picture of each item listed on the chart. Write a one- or two-word description of the item. Write whether the source is primary or secondary. Write the page number where you found each example. The first one has been done for you.

Item	Description	Primary or Secondary?	Page Number
Document	Letter	Primary	12
Artifact			
Photograph			
Book			

Secondary Sources

Now that you know what primary sources are, can you guess what secondary sources are? If you guessed *secondary sources* are made after an event happened, you are right! This textbook is an example of a secondary source. Another example of a secondary source is a newspaper article written today about the first settlers in colonial Maryland. A secondary source is a secondhand account. Sometimes secondary sources discuss facts that were not available at the time of an event.

Reference Materials

Reference books are also secondary sources. They have many kinds of useful information. You might use an atlas or encyclopedia. An atlas is a book of maps. Encyclopedias have information on many different topics listed alphabetically. Newspapers, magazines, and the Internet are also good reference materials.

A textbook is a secondary source because it is written after the events it describes took place. **What historical events does your textbook describe?**

Encyclopedias are secondary sources that contain information about many different subjects. **In what volume of this set of encyclopedias would you look for information about Maryland?**

Point of View

Have you ever enjoyed a movie more than one of your friends did? Just because your friend didn't like the movie as much as you did doesn't mean your friend is wrong.

All people have different points of view. The way someone thinks about something is called *point of view*.

Primary and secondary sources help historians think about history in different ways. They show a place or event from someone else's point of view. Since people are not all the same, they often see and think about things differently. Because of this, historians use many kinds of sources to study history. They study books, pictures, maps, journals, letters, and artifacts to learn about history from many different points of view.

A person's point of view influences how they think about other people, places, and events.
How would this boy's point of view differ from someone's point of view who was not looking through the binoculars?

Fact or Opinion?

Primary and secondary sources can teach you many facts about Maryland history. Facts are things you can prove. Here are some examples of facts:

- The capital of Maryland is Annapolis.
- The Potomac River forms much of the boundary between Maryland and Virginia.
- The largest body of water in Maryland is the Chesapeake Bay.

Facts help you form opinions. Opinions are things you might believe, such as, "Chocolate ice cream is better than vanilla." Opinions express your point of view. Historians like to learn facts before they form opinions about people or events.

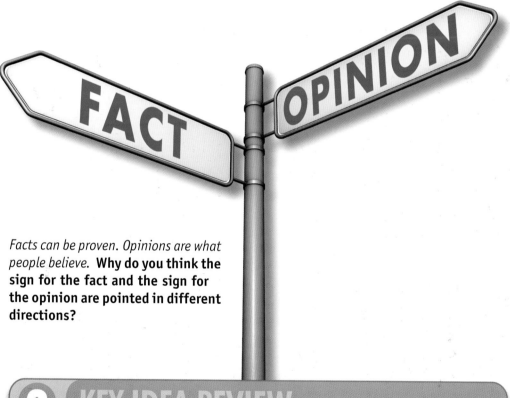

Facts can be proven. Opinions are what people believe. **Why do you think the sign for the fact and the sign for the opinion are pointed in different directions?**

2 KEY IDEA REVIEW

1. Why do historians study the past?
2. What is the difference between a primary and a secondary source?
3. What is point of view?
4. Why do you think point of view matters to historians?

Go to the Source

Compare Two Baltimore Pictures

You can learn a lot about how a place changes over time by comparing an old painting to a modern picture. Both of these pictures show Baltimore. The painting above shows Baltimore in 1752. The photo below shows modern Baltimore.

LOOK	THINK	DECIDE
What similarities do you see in the two pictures?	In what ways has Baltimore grown and changed since the 1752 painting?	What clue in the pictures shows a reason for Baltimore's growth?

Five Themes of Geography

You have learned that historians use tools to study history. Geographers also use tools to study geography. Geographers use what are called the five themes of geography. These five themes help geographers think about geography in different ways.

- **Location:** the location of a place on the Earth's surface
- **Place:** a part of the Earth, which could be a continent, country, region, state, city, village, or area where people do not live
- **Region:** an area that shares one or more things in common, which make it different from surrounding areas (you will learn more about regions in the next lesson)
- **People's Relationship with the Earth:** ways in which humans depend on, adapt to, and change the environment
- **Movement:** the movement of people, goods, and ideas

The five themes of geography are tools geographers use to think about geography. **Can you locate where Maryland is on this globe? Which of the five themes does Maryland's location relate to?**

Tools of Geography

Geographers also use other tools to study geography. These tools include maps, globes, photos, charts, and atlases.

Maps

Maps help geographers see the locations of places in relation to one another.

Can you describe the location of where you live? You know that you live on planet Earth. What else do you know about where you live? Maryland is located on the continent of North America. Continents are very large land areas. They have oceans or seas on many sides. Which oceans touch North America?

Maryland is part of the country of the United States of America. A country is a land region under the control of one government. The country to the north is Canada. The country to the south is Mexico. Find these countries on a map.

Our country is divided into states. Maryland is one of 50 states. Maryland is on the East Coast of the United States next to the Atlantic Ocean. Our neighboring states are Delaware, Pennsylvania, West Virginia, and Virginia. Our nation's capital, Washington, D.C., also borders Maryland.

States are also divided into counties. Within each county there are cities and towns.

Planet
▼
Continent
▼
Country
▼
State
▼
County
▼
City or Town

Where in the World Are We?

Our **planet** is Earth.

Our **continent** is North America.

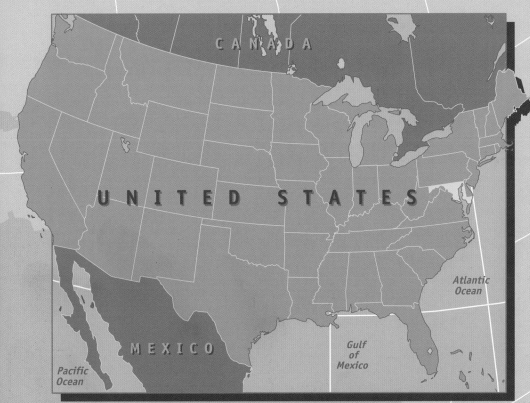

Our **country** is the United States of America.

Our **state** is Maryland.

Reading Maps

Maps help us understand where we are. They help us find our way from one place to another. Did you know that most modern maps begin as photographs? Pictures taken from an airplane, spacecraft, or satellite (an object that circles the Earth in outer space) give mapmakers information they need to create maps.

Maps come in all shapes and sizes. Maybe you have seen a treasure map! Maybe you have looked at a road map your parents use when you go on vacation. The boxes on this page and the next page describe map tools.

Title

The first thing to look for on a map is the title. It is usually at the top. It tells you what the map shows.

Maryland Cities and Towns

Legend, or Key

Mapmakers use *symbols* on maps. The symbols stand for cities, rivers, and other things. The *legend*, or key, explains what the symbols mean.

Legend

- ★ Capital
- ◉ Major U.S. City
- ◎ Large City
- ○ Medium City
- ● Small City or Town
- 〰 River

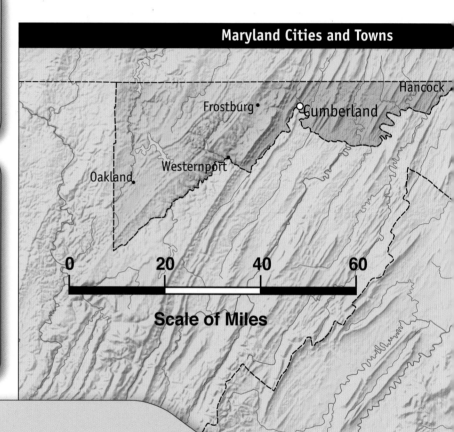

Maryland Cities and Towns

Hancock

Frostburg · ○ Cumberland

Westernport

Oakland ·

0   20   40   60

Scale of Miles

Read a Map

Use the compass, legend, and scale of miles on the map of Maryland to answer the following questions:

1. What direction do you travel to get from Annapolis to Frederick?
2. What direction do you travel to get from La Plata to Havre de Grace?
3. Name three large cities.
4. In what part of the state is Salisbury?
5. Name two medium cities that are close to Washington, D.C.
6. How many miles is it from Chestertown to Oakland?

Scale of Miles

To show how far apart places on a map are, mapmakers use a *scale of miles*. You can use this to measure the distance between places.

On a map, 1 inch might stand for 50 miles or even more on real land.

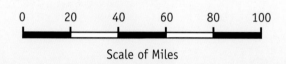

Scale of Miles

Directions

Maps show the directions north, south, east, and west. These are *cardinal directions*. You will find them on a compass rose.

Halfway between north and east is northeast, or NE. Halfway between south and east is southeast, or SE. These are called *intermediate directions*.

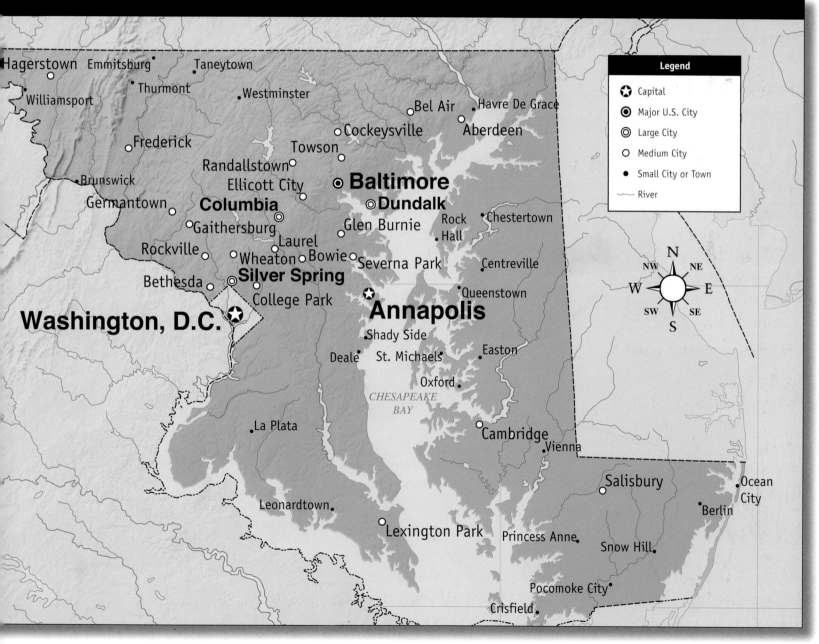

Legend

- ✪ Capital
- ◉ Major U.S. City
- ◎ Large City
- ○ Medium City
- • Small City or Town
- ∿ River

Globes

Another geography tool is a globe. A globe is like a map, but it is round, so you can see the whole Earth at once.

Every place in the world has an exact location using a set of imaginary lines on the Earth. These imaginary lines are called latitude and longitude lines. *Latitude lines* run east and west, and *longitude lines* run north and south. The lines cross each other at certain points called *degrees*. A degree is written as a number with a circle next to it. Degrees help you locate places.

Latitude Lines

The *equator* is at 0 degrees latitude. Other latitude lines run above the equator and below it. These lines are labeled either north (N) or south (S). Is 45 degrees N latitude above or below the equator? If you said above, you are correct because the line is north of the equator.

Longitude Lines

Longitude lines run from the North Pole to the South Pole. Longitude lines are also called *meridians*.

A special longitude line is called the prime meridian. It goes from the North Pole to the South Pole at 0 degrees. Can you find the prime meridian on the globe pictured here? Because some longitude lines are to the right of the prime meridian and some are to the left, longitude lines are labeled east (E) and west (W). Is 15 degrees E longitude right or left of the prime meridian? If you said right, you are correct because it is east of the prime meridian.

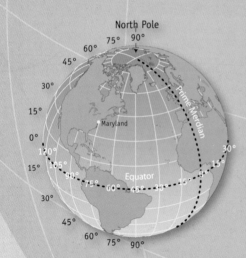

Dividing the World in Half

The equator divides the Earth into two equal halves called *hemispheres*. When it is winter in the Northern Hemisphere, it is summer in the Southern Hemisphere.

Longitude lines also divide the Earth into two parts. These are called the Western and Eastern Hemispheres.

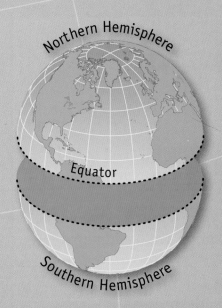

Northern Hemisphere
Equator
Southern Hemisphere

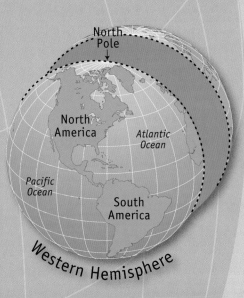

North Pole
North America
Atlantic Ocean
Pacific Ocean
South America
Western Hemisphere

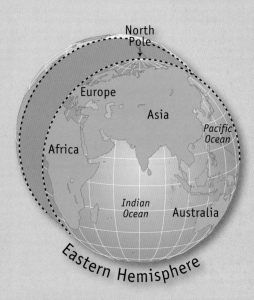

North Pole
Europe
Asia
Africa
Pacific Ocean
Indian Ocean
Australia
Eastern Hemisphere

Additional Tools

Photographs, charts, graphs, and atlases are other tools geographers use. By looking at photos, geographers gather information about places. They might see where there are mountains or what changes people have made to the land.

Charts and graphs compare information. Some charts show number data. For example, a chart might show the number of people living in different states.

Atlases are books of different kinds of maps. For example, an atlas about Maryland might have city maps, climate maps, and transportation maps.

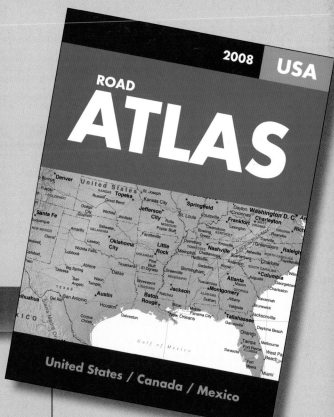

1 KEY IDEA REVIEW

1. Define geography.
2. What tools are used to read a map?
3. What continent is Maryland located on?

LESSON ② Maryland's Land Regions

KEY IDEA

Maryland has three land regions, and each has its own unique features.

WORDS TO UNDERSTAND

climate
drought
elevation
fall line
humid
hurricane
industry
natural resource
population
precipitation
region
temperate

What Are Places Like?

Geographers study what places are like. They study geographic characteristics, which are things in nature and things people make. They also study the people of a place.

Natural Features

Natural features are things like mountains, hills, rivers, and beaches. Animals and plants are also natural features. So is the weather!

Our small state has many different natural features. We have mountains and beaches, forests and wetlands. We have many rivers and the wide Chesapeake Bay.

Many animals live in Maryland, and many plants grow here. Squirrels, chipmunks, rabbits, mice, foxes, deer, opossums, and raccoons live throughout our state. So do birds like robins, cardinals, and sparrows. Many plants also live in most parts of the state. These include common trees like pines, oaks, and maples as well as many smaller plants. Our state flower, the black-eyed Susan, grows throughout Maryland.

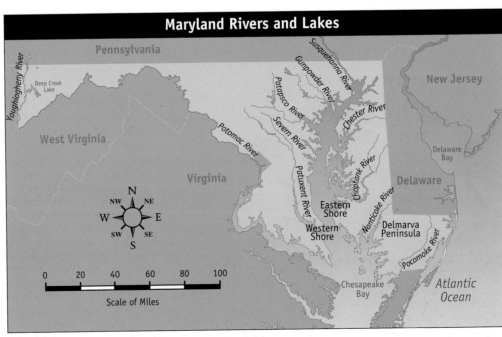

Maryland Rivers and Lakes

Rivers and lakes are natural features. **What river is closest to where you live?**

Chapter 2: Natural Maryland

Human-Made Features

Human-made features are all the things that people have made. Homes, buildings, parking lots, roads, bridges, farms, and even gardens are human-made features. Can you name some human-made features near where you live?

People of Maryland

Human characteristics describe the people of a place. Many different people live in our state. There are old people, young people, and lots of people in between. There are people whose ancestors, or past relatives, came from all parts of the world, including Europe, Africa, Asia, and Latin America. Some of us have Native American ancestors. Most Marylanders speak English. Some speak other languages. Marylanders have many different religions. Overall, Marylanders are well educated.

Jobs People Do

The work people do is an important human characteristic. People use the money they earn to pay for a place to live, food, clothes, and everything else they need.

Marylanders do many different jobs. Some work in factories and some on farms. Many work for the government, in schools, and in hospitals. People in different parts of Maryland also do jobs that use the natural resources of that region. A *natural resource* is something that is found in nature that people use. Examples of natural resources include the land, plants, minerals, and water. Farmers, miners, and people who work in a lumber business do jobs that use natural resources.

People in our state do many different jobs. **What jobs do you think the people in these pictures do?**

What Are Regions?

Areas of land that share common features are called *regions*. Regions can be as large as a country or smaller than a state. For example, Marylanders live in the eastern region of the United States. Some Marylanders live east of the Chesapeake Bay. This region is called the Eastern Shore. Others live west of the Chesapeake Bay in the region sometimes called the Western Shore.

Maryland has city regions and farm regions. In city regions, houses are close together. Streets and highways are often crowded with traffic. There are many factories, businesses, and stores. Farm regions have less traffic, and many people live farther from one another. When they need to shop for clothes or food, they travel to towns and cities nearby.

Climate and Weather

One thing that makes regions different from one another is weather and climate. Do you know the difference between weather and climate? *Climate* is what the weather is like year after year. Weather is what happens each day.

Maryland has many different regions. **How would you describe this region?**

In Maryland, we live in a ***temperate*** zone. This means we are not close to the equator, where it is always hot. We are also not close to the North or South Poles, where it is always cold. In Maryland, we have four seasons. Can you name them?

All parts of Maryland get about the same amount of ***precipitation***, which is rain or snow. Our state gets about 3 to 4 inches of rain a month. When it is cold, we have snow instead of rain. About ten inches of snow equals 1 inch of rain.

Maryland Regions

Our state is divided into three land regions. They are the Atlantic Coastal Plain, the Piedmont Plateau, and the Appalachian region. Although Maryland's regions are the same in many ways, they also have many important differences.

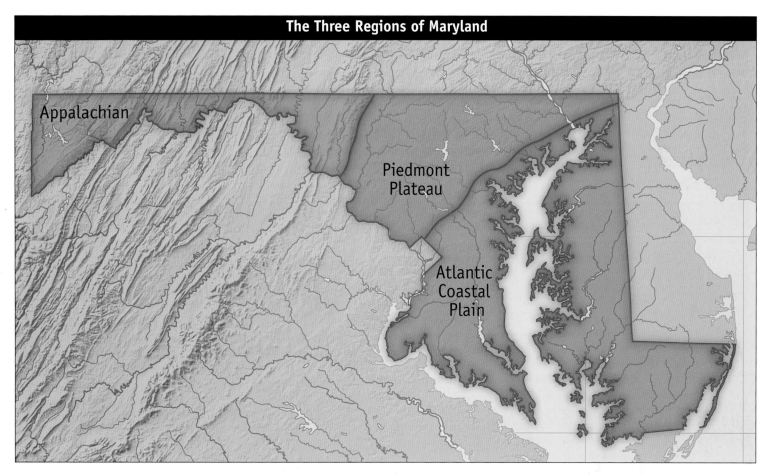

The Three Regions of Maryland

The three land regions of Maryland include the Appalachian, Piedmont Plateau, and Atlantic Coastal Plain. **Which region do you live in?**

Atlantic Coastal Plain Region

The Atlantic Coastal Plain is Maryland's largest region. The Chesapeake Bay divides this region into two smaller regions—the Eastern Shore and the Western Shore. Some of the major cities include Ocean City, Salisbury, Chestertown, Bowie, Annapolis, and the southern and eastern parts of Baltimore City.

Atlantic Coastal Plain region

An unusual geographic feature of the Atlantic Coastal Plain is the Delmarva Peninsula. This piece of land is part of three different states. It is made up of parts of Delaware, parts of Maryland's Eastern Shore, and parts of Virginia.

Natural Features

The land that makes up the Atlantic Coastal Plain is mostly flat. It does not rise very far above sea level. The ocean, bays, beaches, sand dunes, and wetlands are all important natural features of this region. Sand dunes are hills of sand created by the wind. Wetlands are areas that are sometimes covered with water. Many of the waters, like the ocean and the coastal bays, are salty. Other waters, like the Chesapeake Bay, are a mixture of fresh and salt water. Fresh water comes from rivers, such as the Susquehanna, Patapsco, Patuxent, Potomac, Severn, Chester, Choptank, and Nanticoke. These wide and flat rivers flow across the coastal plain and into the Chesapeake Bay.

Another natural feature of the coastal plain is the Aquia aquifer, a big lake under the ground. Aquifers form when rainwater and snow soak into the ground. There are also underground streams. Water from a well comes from an aquifer or an underground stream.

Calvert Cliffs

One of the most unique natural features in Maryland is Calvert Cliffs. Once the cliffs were part of an ancient sea floor under shallow waters. Today they stretch alongside the Chesapeake Bay and reach more than one hundred feet into the sky. Visitors have found fossils, bones, and even sharks' teeth on the beach. Would you be excited to find sharks' teeth that were 5 inches long? Some people have even found bones from whales and dolphins.

The Calvert Cliffs are a very good place to collect fossils and other treasures. **What are some of the items shown in this picture that were found on the beach?**

Hurricane Isabel was a very powerful storm that flooded the streets of Crisfield in 2003. **What are the people in this picture doing?**

Climate

The Atlantic Coastal Plain is the warmest region of Maryland. It has mild winters and hot, humid summers. *Humid* means the air is moist. The climate is mild because the Atlantic Ocean and the Chesapeake Bay are part of the coastal plain. These large bodies of water change temperature slowly, so they slow down temperature changes on the land nearby. Regular rainfall makes the region good for farming.

Sometimes the weather in this region makes life difficult. Dangerous storms called *hurricanes* bring strong winds and heavy rain. Sometimes there are *droughts*, periods when there is very little rain. Many plants die. Farmers suffer.

Minerals, Plants, and Animals

The soils of the Atlantic Coastal Plain are mostly sand, clay, and silt. Silt is made up of sand and very small pieces of rock left behind by water. Sand and clay are used in construction materials.

Some plants grow only in this region. Most are plants that grow in water, such as bay grasses, and plants and trees that grow in very sandy soil, such as the loblolly pine.

Many animals live in the waters and wetlands of the Chesapeake Bay and the coastal plain rivers. The bay is home to oysters, clams, blue crabs, rockfish, turtles, ducks, Canada geese, eagles, and ospreys. Brown pelicans live along the coast during the summer. Wild horses are some of Maryland's most unusual animals. They have been roaming the beaches of Assateague Island for several hundred years.

Ospreys and other birds live near the Chesapeake Bay. **How do you think ospreys catch fish?**

The black-eyed Susan is Maryland's state flower. **Have you ever seen these flowers growing?**

Chesapeake Bay

The Chesapeake Bay is one of our country's most valuable treasures. If you have seen the bay, you know that it is very beautiful. It is also important in many ways. A lot of people earn money by doing jobs that use resources from the bay. Many plants and animals also depend on the bay.

The Chesapeake Bay is really a flooded river valley. Until 10,000 years ago, the Susquehanna River flowed to the ocean, where the bay is now. As glaciers melted at the end of the last ice age, the ocean level rose and flooded the Susquehanna River Valley.

The Chesapeake Bay is a mixture of fresh water from rivers and salt water from the ocean. Like the ocean, the Chesapeake Bay has tides. The ocean's high tide pushes water into the bay. When the ocean's tide goes out, water from the bay rushes after it. This is called low tide. **Have you ever watched the tide roll in?**

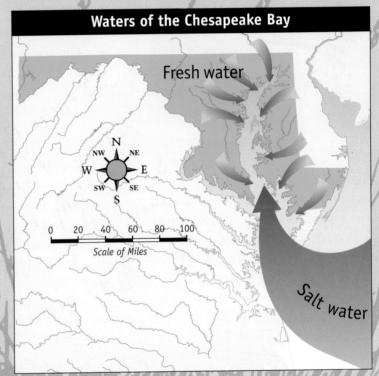

Waters of the Chesapeake Bay

Fresh water

N
NW · NE
W · E
SW · SE
S

0 20 40 60 80 100
Scale of Miles

Salt water

Did you know that there are islands in the Chesapeake Bay? The largest is Kent Island.

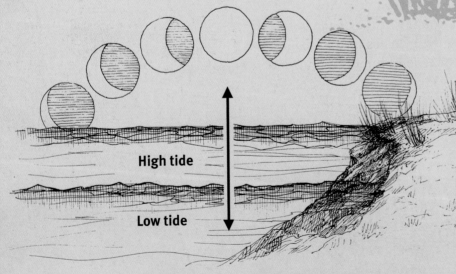

High tide

Low tide

Tides are affected by the moon. When the moon is full, the high tide is very high and the low tide is very low. Between the full moons, the high tides are not quite as high and the low tides are not quite as low.

Chapter 2: Natural Maryland

Keeping the Bay Clean

We eat fish and shellfish from the Chesapeake Bay. Have you ever eaten oysters, clams, or crabs? What about rockfish, bluefish, or perch? These fish eat smaller fish like anchovies and menhaden that also live in the bay. Some small fish eat tiny plants that float in the water.

There are fewer fish and shellfish that live in the bay today than there were 200 years ago. One reason is that many fish and shellfish have been caught. The other reason is that the water is often dirty, which destroys the oxygen that fish and shellfish need to breathe. Dirty water can also block the sun's light. Without sun, underwater plants cannot grow. Grasses that grow in shallow parts of the bay are especially important because fish and shellfish often raise their young there.

All of us can do our part to protect the Chesapeake Bay. What can you do?

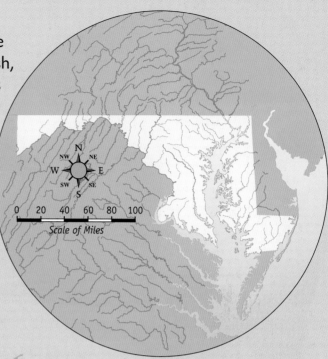

Rivers Flow to the Chesapeake Bay

0   20   40   60   80   100
Scale of Miles

Water flows into the Chesapeake Bay from rivers and streams in many states.
Can you point to the Chesapeake Bay on this map?

Facts About the Bay

The Chesapeake Bay is:
- 200 miles long
- 4 miles wide near Annapolis
- 30 miles wide at its southern end
- made up of 18 trillion gallons of water

Many people fish in the Chesapeake Bay.
Why do you think it is important to them for the bay to be clean?

The Chesapeake Bay Bridge is a human-made feature. **What other human-made features might you see in this picture if it had been taken at a different time of day?**

Human-Made Features

There are many human-made features spread across the Atlantic Coastal Plain. You can see many examples in Ocean City. That land used to be mostly beaches and sand dunes. Today, it is a resort town with hotels, stores, and restaurants.

Another important human-made feature of this region is the Chesapeake Bay Bridge. This 4-mile-long bridge allows cars to cross the bay. Before it was built, the Eastern Shore was mostly farmland and small towns.

This statue of John Smith, who explored the area around the Chesapeake Bay, is a human-made feature. **How do you think the person who created this statue wanted people to member John Smith?**

The Port of Baltimore is also a human-made feature. It is located on the calm water of the Patapsco River, on the southern side of Baltimore City. The port has docks for boats, yards where boats can be repaired, and large areas of paved land where goods can be loaded and unloaded. Train tracks and roads come all the way to the harbor so that goods can be easily moved between trains or trucks and ships. This human-made feature is very important for Maryland's economy.

People of the Atlantic Coastal Plain

Many people live on the Atlantic Coastal Plain. Descendants of some of the first people to come to America from Europe and Africa live here. Today, people with families from Asia, the Caribbean, Africa, and Latin America also live in Maryland. Native Americans also make up a very small part of the population. *Population* is the number of people living in an area.

Jobs People Do

Some jobs on the Atlantic Coastal Plain are tied to the natural features of the region. Some people do jobs that use the ocean and Chesapeake Bay. They catch crabs, oysters, and fish to sell across the United States. Some people build, sell, and repair boats. The coastal plain's wide, flat rivers make it a good place for ships to dock. Lots of people work in the region's ports, especially the Port of Baltimore.

Farming is very important in this region. Farmers grow corn, tomatoes, soybeans, and other crops here. Farmers raise chickens on the Eastern Shore. Have you enjoyed local summer peaches or watermelon?

Tourism is also very important to the coastal plain. Visitors enjoy the ocean, the Chesapeake Bay, and many interesting towns. Visitors buy food from local farmers and fishermen. Many Marylanders work in hotels and restaurants here.

Water taxis carry people from one side of Baltimore's harbor to the other. **Have you ever ridden in a water taxi?**

Many major cities along the East Coast of the United States are located in the Atlantic Coastal Plain. Baltimore is one of these. **What human-made and natural features do you see in this picture?**

The Piedmont Plateau cuts across the central part of Maryland. More than half of Maryland's population lives in this region. Some of its big cities include Gaithersburg, Frederick, Rockville, Columbia, Westminster, and northern and western Baltimore.

Piedmont Plateau region

Natural Features

The Piedmont Plateau has gently rolling hills and valleys. There are dairy farms and crop fields. Before people settled here, the area was mostly forest.

Because the Piedmont Plateau is higher than the coastal plain, rivers and streams in the area flow downhill quickly until they reach the flat plain. The place where the last steep drop occurs is called the fall line. At that point, because of the steep drop, there is a waterfall. An imaginary line connecting all those last waterfalls of the rivers is called the *fall line*.

Many of Maryland's major rivers flow through the Piedmont Plateau. The Potomac, Patuxent, Patapsco, Gunpowder, and Susquehanna all flow downhill until they reach the flat coastal plain and empty into the Chesapeake Bay.

The Piedmont has fewer wetlands than the Atlantic Coastal Plain. Unlike the salty coastal wetlands, the Piedmont wetlands contain fresh water. Plants that grow in the fresh water wetlands provide a home for birds and other animals. They also help keep the water clean.

Climate

Like the rest of Maryland, the Piedmont Plateau is a temperate zone. Its higher elevation means it has colder winters, with more snow and ice, than the coastal plain. *Elevation* is how high the land is above sea level. Another reason the winters are colder is that most of the region is farther from the ocean and the Chesapeake Bay.

The Great Falls of the Potomac River are near Washington, D.C. **Would the Great Falls be good for rafting?**

Chapter 2: Natural Maryland

Granite is sometimes used in building materials.

People ride horses in Maryland today for fun. In the past, people used horses to do work. **What types of work do you think horses did?**

Minerals, Plants, and Animals

The Piedmont Plateau region has many minerals, including granite, limestone, sandstone, and slate. They are sometimes used as building materials.

Many trees and plants grow in this region. Oak, maple, and tulip poplar trees grow here. Blueberries, strawberries, milkweed plants, and sunflowers are also found here.

Most of the animals in this region live in other parts of Maryland, too. Coyotes have recently been moving here. Some fish in this region live in both fresh and salt water. Shad and herring are often born in the fresh water rivers. After swimming downstream to the Atlantic Coastal Plain, they spend most of their lives in salty waters. When they are ready to lay their eggs, they return to the fresh water stream where they were born.

Monarch butterflies fly all the way from Maryland to Mexico to spend the winter. Their offspring return to Maryland in the summer. **Have you ever seen a monarch butterfly?**

Lesson 2: Maryland's Land Regions

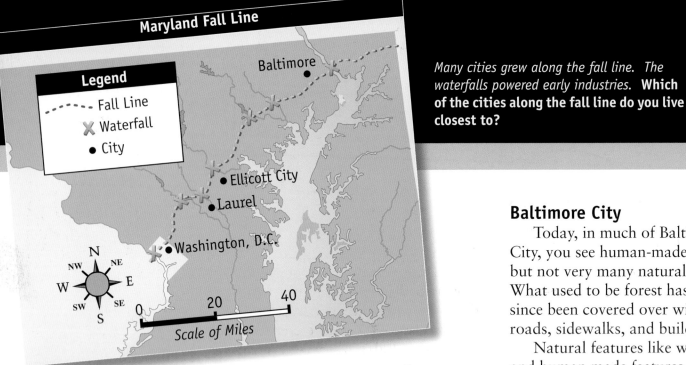

Maryland Fall Line

Legend
- - - - Fall Line
✗ Waterfall
● City

Baltimore

Ellicott City

Laurel

Washington, D.C.

N NE NW W E SW SE S

0   20   40

Scale of Miles

Many cities grew along the fall line. The waterfalls powered early industries. **Which of the cities along the fall line do you live closest to?**

Human-Made Features

Some of Maryland's largest cities were built along the fall line, where fast-flowing rivers could power early factories. Baltimore, Ellicott City, and Laurel all grew up along these waterfalls. Today, modern businesses have replaced many older businesses. Large highways, like the Baltimore and Washington Beltways and Interstate 95, cross the region.

Shipping is an important industry in Baltimore. Baltimore's port grew because of the industries and crops of the Piedmont, just to the north and west. **What human-made features do ports have?**

Baltimore City

Today, in much of Baltimore City, you see human-made features but not very many natural features. What used to be forest has long since been covered over with roads, sidewalks, and buildings.

Natural features like waterfalls and human made features like the port helped Baltimore City grow. It grew into the largest city in Maryland, with the most industries, the most important port, and the most people. An ***industry*** is a group of similar businesses.

The People of the Piedmont

The Piedmont Plateau region has the greatest population density. That means that the region has the most people for the amount of land. People live close together.

The people of this region have come from many different countries. Even today, more people come to this region of Maryland than to other parts of our state.

People have come from many different countries to live in the Piedmont Plateau region. **Do you know anyone who has come to Maryland from another country?**

Jobs People Do

The jobs in the Piedmont Plateau region have changed over the years. Many industries have grown up all across the area. For many years, steel mills, car factories, and shipping were major businesses. Today, people still work in factories and at the ports, but technology companies have also grown in importance. Many people work with computers. Others are scientists. Many people work in the medical field. Other people work for the government in offices in Maryland and in Washington, D.C.

Even though there are fewer farms and farmers than there used to be, wheat, corn, fruits, and vegetables are still grown here. Dairy farms are important, too. Today, local farmers sell what they grow at farmers markets all across the state. People like buying food that they know is locally grown and fresh.

▶ Farmer's market photo by Suzanne Chapelle

Some Maryland farmers sell their fruits and vegetables at farmers markets like this one. **Do you see any vegetables you like to eat in this picture?**

Appalachian Region

The Appalachian region is the smallest of Maryland's three regions. It stretches across Washington, Allegany, and Garrett Counties in the western part of Maryland. Hagerstown, Cumberland, and Frostburg are important cities.

Appalachian region

Natural Features

The Appalachian region has some dramatic natural features. The green forests of the Blue Ridge Mountains are one of four smaller areas that make up the region. The Great Valley, the Ridge and Valley, and the Allegheny Plateau make up the other three. The Appalachian region has more forests than Maryland's other regions.

The Appalachian region has the highest land in Maryland. The mountains there are part of the chain of the Appalachian Mountains that stretches from eastern Canada south to Alabama. As you go west, the mountains get higher and higher. Backbone Mountain, in Garrett County, is the highest mountain in the state. It rises 3,360 feet above sea level.

Most rivers and streams in the Appalachian region flow into the Potomac River, then into the Chesapeake Bay, and end up in the Atlantic Ocean. A few rivers on the far western side of the mountains flow into the Mississippi River and then the Gulf of Mexico. One of these is the fast-flowing Youghiogheny (YOK·ah·gay·nee). The fast-flowing rivers flow down the sides of mountains.

The Appalachian region has four seasons. **Which season is shown in this picture?**

42

The winters in the Appalachian region are very cold. **What is this man doing?**

Climate

The Appalachian region has the coldest weather and deepest snow in Maryland. Its high elevation and distance from the ocean and the Chesapeake Bay are the main reasons for this. The cold weather lasts longer and the summers are shorter and not as warm as in other regions of the state. Cold winds blow across the tops of the mountains.

Minerals, Plants, and Animals

A very important mineral in the Appalachian region is coal. The coal is used by industries for fuel. It is also used to make electricity. Your great-grandparents may have heated their homes with coal. Natural gas, another important fuel, is also found here.

Plants and trees must be able to survive the cold winters here. Because there is a shorter summer, some crops cannot be grown here. Apples and wheat grow well here. The region also has dairy farms.

This region has many of the same animals that live all across the state. Coyotes and black bears live here. Some people say that too many bears come near homes and campgrounds. Some people want to get rid of the bears. Others say people could keep the bears away by storing their garbage and other food that attract the bears in a safe place, where the bears are not able to get to them.

Crops like apples grow well in the Appalachian region. **Have you ever eaten a juicy red apple?**

Most of the bears in Maryland live in the Appalachian region. **Have you ever seen a bear while you were camping?**

People enjoy outdoor activities in the Appalachian region. **What outdoor activity is this man doing?**

▲ Photo of bear by Middleton Evans

Many people enjoy coming to this region for a vacation. People enjoy ski trails and ice rinks. Maryland's largest fresh water lake is located here. Deep Creek Lake is a human-made lake. Many people love to come here year-round to fish, hunt, hike, and enjoy the region's snow. Vacation homes, lodges, and hotels provide places for people to stay.

Human-Made Features

Even though there are fewer people who live in the Appalachian region than in other parts of our state, humans have left their mark. People have built offices, factories, schools, and homes in the cities of Hagerstown and Cumberland and in smaller towns. Railroads pass through here. Today, a new highway, Interstate 68, connects many of the region's smaller cities and towns.

People like to visit the Appalachian region for vacation. **What activities might visitors do in the woods in winter?**

Deep Creek Lake is human made. **What other human-made features do you see in this picture?**

People of the Appalachian Region

Native tribes were the first to make their homes in the forests of the Appalachian region. Later, many people passed through here on their way farther west. Some pioneers stayed. They cleared the forests and built homes and farms for their families. Even today, this region does not have as many people as other regions in Maryland.

Jobs People Do

People living in the Appalachian region do many different jobs. A lot of the jobs are closely connected with the natural features or the natural resources of the area. Some people continue to farm in the Great Valley.

Some men follow in the footsteps of their fathers and work deep in the coal mines. Coal mining is a dangerous job. Mine accidents can result in cave-ins that bury workers. The dust from coal can cause lung problems.

Other people in western Maryland help produce natural gas, harvest trees for timber, and work in the tourist industry.

Farmers use Belgian workhorses on some farms in the Appalachian region. **What work do you suppose these horses do on this farm in Hagerstown?**

2) KEY IDEA REVIEW

1. What are the three regions of Maryland?
2. Name two human-made features and two natural features of Maryland.
3. List Maryland's land regions from smallest to largest.

The timber industry is important in western Maryland. **What products are made from timber?**

KEY IDEA

The movement of people, goods, and ideas as well as relationships have influenced our world and state.

WORDS TO UNDERSTAND

conserve
culture
ecosystem
pollution
predator
settlement

Geography affects where people choose to live.

On the Move

An important part of geography is studying how people, goods, and ideas move. People have moved and continue to move to different places and sometimes even to different countries. When people move, they take the things that belong to them as well as their ideas and ways of life with them.

Choosing Where to Live

Geography affects where and how people live. People in the past and many people today live near water. Why do you think people choose to live near water? People need water to drink and bathe in as well as to grow crops and give to animals to drink. People choose to live on flat land more often than in mountains. Flat land is easier to build homes on and to farm. Many people choose to live where it is not too hot or too cold.

What Do You Think?

Many people build their homes on or near a floodplain. A floodplain is land that lies right next to a river. When rivers overflow their banks, the extra water spills out onto the floodplain. Do you think it is good or bad to build a home on a floodplain?

When choosing where to live, people also consider what resources are available. Some of the first Europeans to come to North America wanted to trap animals to get their furs. Today, many of the jobs people do also depend on the resources available in the area. As you read in the last lesson, some jobs related to natural resources include mining, farming, and fishing.

The First Europeans to Settle in Maryland

When the first European settlers came to Maryland, they looked for a good place to live. They wanted to live where the climate and soil would be good for growing crops, and they wanted to be close to water.

The Europeans created a *settlement* next to a Yaocomico Indian village along a river near the Chesapeake Bay. The Europeans set up homes. The Yaocomico people taught the settlers about the land and its resources. They taught the settlers how to grow crops like corn and where to fish. The Indians and the Europeans shared many ideas and traded with one another.

The first Europeans came to Maryland because they hoped for a better life. They wanted more freedoms and opportunities. Over the centuries, people have continued to come to Maryland for these same reasons.

The first Europeans to settle in Maryland and the Indians shared goods and ideas.
What are the people exchanging in this painting?

New Ways to Move

The ways that people and goods move have changed and continue to change. The first Europeans who came to America sailed across the Atlantic Ocean on ships. During their first years in America, they traveled on foot, by horse, and by boat. Ships carried goods from England to America and from one place on the East Coast to another.

It gradually got easier for people and goods to move across the country. People built roads, canals, and railroads. People usually traveled to places that they could reach easily, along rivers or along roads or train lines. They built new towns on the banks of these rivers and near roads and train lines.

Today, people and goods continue to move. People move around the world in cars, trains, ships, and airplanes. Products from Maryland's farms and factories and from the Chesapeake Bay are shipped all over the world. People in other states and countries buy these products and Marylanders buy products from them.

How Ideas Move

When people move, they take their ideas with them. When the first Europeans came to Maryland, they brought their culture with them. *Culture* includes people's beliefs, practices, and ways of life. In recent years, other newcomers have brought their cultures with them, too.

Ideas and information travel quickly around the world today. Televisions, computers, and cell phones make it easy to share information. You may read a book written by someone who lives in a different country. You may watch a movie or a TV show made in a different part of the world. Maybe you have a pen pal or a friend you e-mail in another state or country.

Today, ideas and information move around the world quickly.
What is this girl using to communicate?

All parts of nature work together in an ecosystem. **What parts of nature are working together in the ecosystem shown here?**

Relationships

People have relationships with family, friends, and neighbors. We spend time with one another. We depend on one another. With whom do you have relationships in your life?

Did you know that people also have a relationship with the Earth? We all depend on the Earth for resources. The natural world gives us water to drink, food to eat, and air to breathe.

One of people's most important relationships is with the ecosystems of the world. We are all part of an ecosystem. An **ecosystem** is a community of living things. An ecosystem can include people, animals, plants, soil, water, and air that all interact with each other. Every living creature is part of an ecosystem. An ecosystem can be large or small. The whole Earth is one huge ecosystem. One small patch of woods can also be an ecosystem.

What Do You Think?

Why do you think it is important to have good relationships with the people in your life? Why do you think it is important to have a good relationship with the Earth?

ECOSYSTEMS

Each part of an ecosystem affects all the other parts. Each part does its own special job. For example, some animals called *predators* eat smaller animals. Other animals eat only plants. Plants depend on soil that is made rich by dead plants and animals. Rich soil helps plants grow. People depend on ecosystems to survive.

AIR

Clean air is part of a healthy ecosystem. However, air *pollution* from factories, power plants, cars, and airplanes makes the air dirty. They put gases and dust into the air. Do you know kids who have asthma? Do they have trouble breathing when the air is badly polluted?

WATER

Clean water is another part of a healthy ecosystem. We need clean water to survive.

Water pollution can make us sick. It can kill the animals that live in our streams, rivers, lakes, bays, and oceans. Many things like trash and chemicals can pollute water. Some companies let poisonous chemicals flow into our water. Almost everything that is washed from the street down a storm drain goes into our rivers. What kinds of things from the street might wind up in a river? Where does that water go from there?

Trash Can Hurt Animals

Did you know that a balloon that blows away or a plastic bag that someone throws on the ground can be a real danger to dolphins, whales, and turtles? They might eat the plastic, mistaking it for a yummy jellyfish. The animals may die when the plastic sticks in their stomachs. What do you think we should do with our trash?

Chapter 3

Native Americans were the first people to live in North America. The first Indians came from Asia to North America thousands of years ago. They built villages near rivers. They hunted animals and gathered plants and seeds to eat. They learned where to find or how to make everything they needed in nature. Later, people learned to farm the land.

Some Native Americans still live in Maryland today. They are part of our state's rich history.

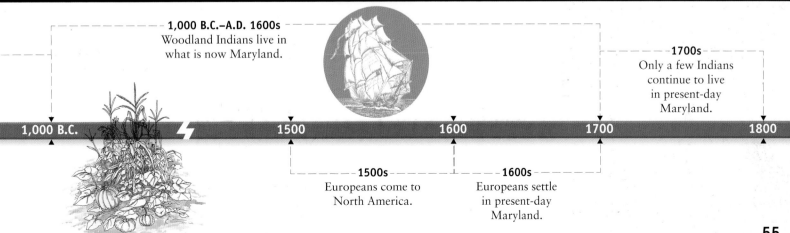

1,000 B.C.–A.D. 1600s
Woodland Indians live in what is now Maryland.

1700s
Only a few Indians continue to live in present-day Maryland.

1,000 B.C.   1500   1600   1700   1800

1500s
Europeans come to North America.

1600s
Europeans settle in present-day Maryland.

KEY IDEA

Paleo-Indians and Archaic Indians lived in Maryland before history was written down.

WORDS TO UNDERSTAND

atlatl
extinct
glacier
hunter-gatherer
paleo
prehistoric
theory

Moving to North America

Many scientists have a *theory*, or possible explanation based on facts, about how the first people came to North America. Scientists believe they arrived on foot thousands of years ago. This period was called the Ice Age because the climate was so cold. The level of the oceans was much lower than it is today. The water was so low that a land bridge connected Asia to North America. Today, that land bridge is beneath the sea.

We do not know much about the people who lived here during prehistoric times. *Prehistoric* means before history was written down. Scientists get information about how people lived and about what kinds of tools they used from artifacts. However, most artifacts do not give information about what kind of language the people spoke or what their beliefs were.

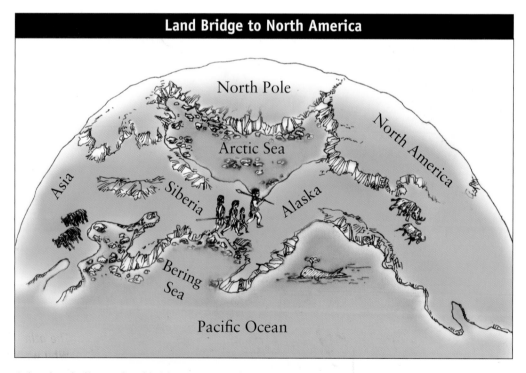

Land Bridge to North America

Scientists believe a land bridge connected Asia to North America long ago. **How might the people have moved from Asia to North America?**

Paleo-Indians

We call the first people who lived in North America Paleo-Indians. *Paleo* means ancient, or very old. Scientists believe the people reached the land we call Maryland about 14,000 years ago. At the time, large, slow-moving sheets of ice called *glaciers* covered much of the land north of Maryland. The area where the Chesapeake Bay is today was a river valley.

The climate was cold. Giant animals, such as woolly mammoths and saber-toothed tigers, lived in the grasslands that spread across the land. The Paleo-Indians were *hunter-gatherers*. They hunted the huge animals as well as smaller animals like white-tailed deer. They also caught fish from the rivers. They gathered berries, nuts, leaves, and roots from plants.

Paleo-Indians made tools from stone. They used very hard stones to chip other stones until they had sharp edges. They made knives and points for their spears. They made scrapers to scrape animal hides they wore as clothing. They also made a tool called an *atlatl* that helped hunters throw their spears.

Saber-toothed tigers lived in North America. **What was the landscape like where this tiger lived?**

The atlatl helped Archaic hunters throw a spear. **Why would the atlatl have been better for hunting than just a spear?**

The Ice Age gradually came to an end. **What do you think happened to the big glaciers that covered the northern parts of North America?**

The Climate Warms

As time passed, the climate in North America began to change. The temperature got warmer, and glaciers began to melt. The water formed new rivers and lakes. Water filled the Susquehanna River Valley and formed the Chesapeake Bay. More trees grew.

Many giant animals became *extinct*. They may not have been able to live in the warmer climate, or perhaps the people hunted too many of them. After the big animals died out, deer became a major source of food for the people. People also began to harvest shellfish like oysters and clams from the Chesapeake Bay.

Archaic Indians

As the natural world changed, people's lifestyles also changed. The Archaic Indians lived after the Paleo-Indians. Archaic Indians developed new skills. Families moved around in search of food but also still gathered plants for food. They ground seeds and nuts into flour to make a food that was like bread.

Like Paleo-Indians, Archaic Indians lived in small groups. They traveled around to get food that was available at different times of the year. The people made spears, fish traps, nets, and canoes. They carved bowls from a soft rock called soapstone.

❶ KEY IDEA REVIEW

1. How do scientists learn about prehistoric people?
2. Write two facts about Paleo-Indians.
3. Write two facts about Archaic Indians.

Woodland Indians

Over time, the natural world and the lifestyle of the people changed again. The people who lived in the eastern United States about 3,000 years ago are called Woodland Indians. We know more about Woodland Indians than we do about earlier peoples who lived in what is now Maryland. Since the Woodland Indians lived in recent centuries, more things that the people made are still around for us to study. The first Europeans to arrive in North America also wrote about the people they met here.

The Woodland Indians' most important new idea was farming. The people still hunted and gathered food, but they began to grow food, too. Because they grew crops, they could settle down in one place. They no longer had to travel so much to find enough to eat. Since there was more food, the population grew.

Villages, Tribes, and Nations

Most Woodland Indians lived in villages. Like our towns and cities, Woodland villages had names. The people of each village were part of a larger group called a tribe. Members of a tribe shared a way of life and a common language. Many tribes spoke similar languages. Sometimes these tribes joined together in larger groups called nations.

KEY IDEA

The Woodland Indians had a system of government and trade that helped the tribes thrive.

WORDS TO UNDERSTAND

ally
ancestor
barter
council
govern
wampum

Nation
Tribe
Village

Most Woodland Indians lived in villages. **From looking at this picture, what can you describe about life in a village?**

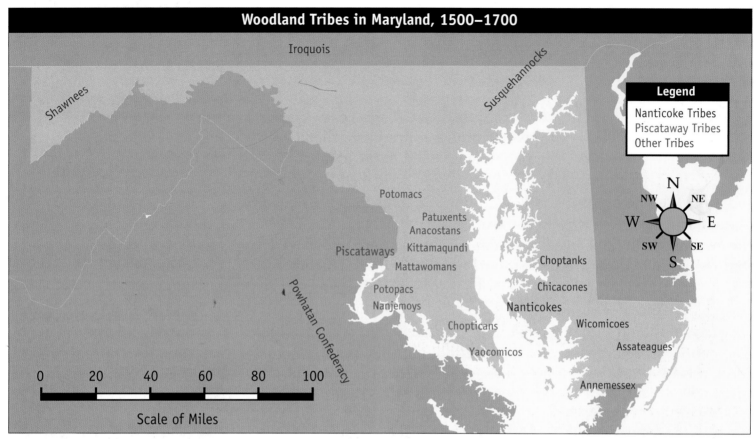

Woodland Tribes in Maryland, 1500–1700

Iroquois

Shawnees

Susquehannocks

Potomacs

Patuxents
Anacostans

Piscataways   Kittamaqundi

Mattawomans

Potopacs

Nanjemoys

Choptanks

Chicacones

Nanticokes

Chopticans

Wicomicoes

Yaocomicos

Assateagues

Annemessex

Powhatan Confederacy

Legend
Nanticoke Tribes
Piscataway Tribes
Other Tribes

N NE NW W E SW SE S

0 20 40 60 80 100
Scale of Miles

There were many Woodland tribes that lived in Maryland during this period.
Which tribe lived closest to where you live today?

Native Americans Today

Native Americans live in Maryland today. Several Piscataway groups live in southern Maryland. They plan events and share their culture. A Nanticoke group lives in Delaware. In recent years, Lumbee Indians from North Carolina moved to Baltimore City to work. They, too, want to preserve their culture and share it with other Marylanders. Many people across the state have Indian ancestors. Do you? An *ancestor* is a past relative.

Woodland Tribes

In the land we call Maryland, there were several Woodland tribes. The largest group on the Eastern Shore was the Nanticoke (Nahn·tih·KOHK) tribe. Smaller tribes became their *allies*. They agreed to protect each other and work together.

The largest tribe on the Western Shore was the Piscataway. They also had smaller tribes as allies. At certain times in history, Shawnee Indians lived in western Maryland. The Piscataways, Nanticokes, and Shawnees all spoke languages in the Algonquin (Ahl·GAHWN·kwihn) family.

Farther north were the Susquehannocks (Suhs·kweh·HAN·ahks). Their language was different from those of other tribes. It was part of the Iroquois (Ir·oh·KOI) language family. However, the Susquehannocks were not part of the large Iroquois nation.

Susquehannocks built villages along the Susquehanna River in what is now Pennsylvania. They also had some villages along the Potomac River.

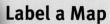

Label a Map

Many places and landforms in Maryland are still called by their Indian names. These names often describe the place. Here are a few examples:

Wicomico = pleasant dwelling place
Nanticoke = tidal river or waves
Chesapeake = great shellfish bay
Potomac = where the goods are brought in
Kittamaqundi = place of the Great Old Beaver (the Piscataway ruler was called the Great Old Beaver)
Susquehanna = smooth-flowing stream
Catoctin = speckled mountain
Lonaconing = where there is a beautiful summit
Youghiogheny = a muddy, flowing stream

Complete these steps:

1. Copy the map of Maryland below onto your own paper.
2. Choose five of the places or landforms with Indian names listed above and label them on your map. You will need to use another map or the Internet to help you.
3. Choose one of the items labeled on your map and write a paragraph about why you think it was given that name.

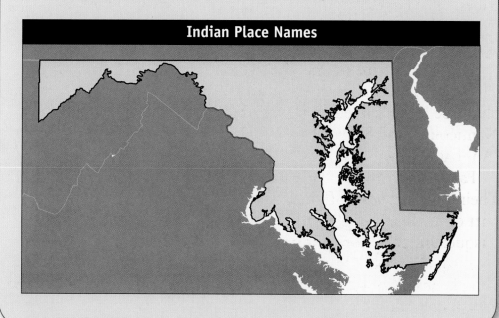

Indian Place Names

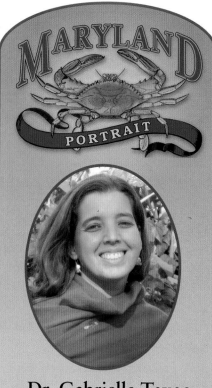

Dr. Gabrielle Tayac

Gabrielle Tayac is the granddaughter of a chief of Piscataways in Maryland. Her grandfather worked hard to save the culture of the Piscataways. Many had died or left Maryland by the 1700s.

Tayac teaches people about Indian history. She is a historian at the National Museum of the American Indian in Washington, D.C.

Tayac wrote a book about her 11-year-old cousin called *Meet Naiche: A Native Boy from the Chesapeake Bay Area*. The book follows Naiche through a day at school and as he takes part in Indian society.

Many Indian groups had a war council and a peace council. **Do you think this is a painting of a war council or a peace council?**

Governing the Tribe

Tribes had different ways of **governing**, or ruling, themselves. A ruler, sometimes called a chief, was the head of a tribe. Rulers were also called by other names. Most tribes had a peace council and a war council. A **council** is a group of people that discusses issues.

The Nanticokes and Piscataways called their local leader a "werowance." Sometimes a woman served as the werowance. A "tayac" was the leader of several towns or tribes.

In all Woodland tribes, women had some rights and powers. They often helped make decisions. The village councils discussed issues until they could agree on what was best. Rulers had to talk to priests, warriors, and the tribal councils before they could make important decisions or wage war.

War

Tribes did not always get along with one another. Sometimes two or more tribes wanted to use the same land. When this happened, they went to war.

The Susquehannocks were known as fierce fighters. When they hunted, they traveled into territory that the Nanticokes and the Piscataways considered theirs. Sometimes wars broke out between the tribes.

Indians lost family members when they went to war. Some people were captured. Prisoners often became slaves. Sometimes a prisoner was given to a family that had lost a member during the fighting. These prisoners had to do the dead person's work.

What Do You Think ?

Why do you think the Woodland Indians had two different councils—one for peace and one for war?

Trade

The Woodland people often traveled a long way to trade with their neighbors. The Shawnees had copper jewelry and knives. The Piscataways and Nanticokes had shells. Tribes traded, or *bartered*, for items they needed or wanted.

For example, let's imagine your tribe has a lot of clay pots. But you do not have stones for making spearheads. Tribes from other places have stones. How can you get them? You can barter for them. You can give the other tribes your pots in exchange for their stones.

Woodland tribes often traded for *wampum*. These were beads made of clam and oyster shells. Many Indians used wampum like we use money today. Shawnees were eager to trade their copper goods for wampum.

The people often traveled in canoes along the rivers and up and down the Chesapeake Bay. Sometimes people walked along trails cut through the forest. Some of the early footpaths followed animal paths. Some paths later became colonial roads. Many roads today still follow the routes of old Indian trails.

Woodland tribes used wampum beads to pay for things they needed and wanted. **What were wampum beads made out of?**

2 KEY IDEA REVIEW

1. Describe the role of the council in the government of the Woodland Indians.
2. Why did tribes go to war?
3. How did trade help the Woodland Indians survive and grow?

Woodland Indians Use the Land

Woodland tribes were not all the same, but they did share a similar way of life. They met their needs in similar ways. To survive, they needed shelter, food, and water. They needed protection from their enemies. They needed clothing to keep warm. They needed tools to help them do their work. The Indians knew how to use natural materials to meet their needs.

Villages

Most Woodland Indians lived in small villages. Villages were made up of about 10 to 30 homes. The people built villages near a river or stream, often on high land, so floods would not wash away their homes. They built their villages near groves of trees. The trees kept the village hidden from enemies. Sometimes men built a *palisade*, or high fence, around the village for protection. Women planted fields near the village. During hunting season, everyone moved into temporary homes in the forest to be closer to the animals.

Woodland tribes used things from nature to meet their needs. **How are the people in this picture using nature to meet their needs?**

Woodland Indians lived in homes called witchotts. At Historic St. Mary's City, you can see this re-creation of an Indian village. **Can you describe what witchotts looked like and what materials were used to make the homes?**

Shelters

Woodland Indians lived in wigwams or longhouses, which they called witchotts (whit·CHAHTS). Their homes were made of wood, bark, and grasses. The village leader usually had the biggest home.

There was not much furniture inside the homes. Men built platforms around the walls. Women covered these with grass mats and animal skins. Families sat and slept on the platforms.

The people built a fire in the center of the wigwam. The fire made a thick layer of smoke near the top of the building that kept insects and other pests away. When it rained or snowed, families covered the hole. The homes were hot and smoky. Families cooked outside and also ate outdoors most of the time.

Water

People built villages near a river or stream. Rivers and streams gave the people plenty of water to drink, to bathe in, and to catch fish to eat. Birds and animals came to the water to drink, so hunting was good there. The people also traveled in canoes on the rivers. It was faster than walking across the land.

What Do You Think ?

We still need water to survive. Why are some cities not built close to rivers and streams today?

A Step-by-Step Wigwam

1 To build a wigwam, the people cut down straight, young trees called saplings. They trimmed off the branches. Then they dug holes in the ground. They put the saplings in the holes to hold them in place.

2 Next, the people bent the saplings over and lashed them together with cord, vines, or animal skins to make the frame.

3 Finally, the people covered the frame with bark or mats made of grasses and reeds. They left a door and a hole in the top so the smoke from the fire could escape.

Food

Woodland Indians ate many different kinds of foods. They ate foods that came from the land. The men and older boys of the village hunted deer, rabbits, and squirrels. They also brought home birds, such as pigeons and wild turkeys. They caught fish in rivers throughout present-day Maryland. In the Chesapeake Bay, they gathered oysters, crabs, and clams.

Near modern Hagerstown, there was a small, grassy prairie. This was the only place in what is now Maryland where buffalo lived and could be hunted.

Women and children gathered wild berries. It must have been a special treat to find sweet berries that were ripe only a few weeks during the spring and summer. Women and children also gathered acorns and chestnuts that grew on oak and chestnut trees. People ate roots and leaves. Have you ever picked berries or gathered nuts? Have you ever eaten leaves? If you have eaten lettuce or spinach, then you have!

Woodland Indians ate plants and animals. **What are the people in this picture doing to get food?**

Men hunted animals for food for their families. **What weapon are these men using to hunt?**

Crops

Woodland Indians grew much of their own food. *Agriculture*, or using the land to grow food, was a key reason the Woodland people survived. Since almost all the land was covered with forests, men had to clear land to plant their fields. Sometimes they started fires to kill trees where they wanted to plant. They also killed trees by *girdling* them. They did this by making a cut all the way around the tree.

After a piece of land was cleared, the women planted crops. They started by planting a small hill of corn. When the corn started to grow, they planted beans or peas that would climb the cornstalks. Beans added nitrogen into the soil, which helped the corn to grow.

Girdling a Tree

When you girdle a tree, you cut through the bark and the layer of the tree beneath the bark. The second layer is where nutrients flow from the roots up through the tree. If that layer is cut away, the tree will die. Girdling trees was one way Woodland Indians cleared a large area of land.

Chapter 4

There was a time when Europeans did not know North and South America existed. They learned about these lands after European explorers sailed here.

Europeans set up many colonies in the "New World." A lot of people took a great risk to leave their homes and settle in the new colonies. They left Europe for many different reasons.

Native Americans and the new settlers had many conflicts, but sometimes they got along.

1632
The Maryland Charter of 1632 establishes Maryland as a colony.

THE CHARTER OF MARYLAND. CHARLES By the Grace of GOD, King of England, Scotland, France and Ireland, Defender of the Faith &c. To all to whom these Presents shall come Greeting. WHEREAS...

1634
- The *Ark* and the *Dove* arrive at the Maryland colony.
- St. Mary's City is founded.

1729
The town of Baltimore is started.

1650

1700

1750

1631
A trading post is built at Kent Island.

1642
Thirteen Africans are brought to Maryland.

1645–1646
The Time of Troubles

1649
The Toleration Act is passed.

1695
The capital of the colony is moved from St. Mary's City to Annapolis.

KEY IDEA

Europeans came to North America to take control of the land to increase the power of their nations.

WORDS TO UNDERSTAND

colony
conquer
convert
disease
missionary
raw material
starvation

Like other explorers, Christopher Columbus set off from Spain on explorations to find new trade routes. **Who do you think the people on shore are?**

The "New World"

To understand how Maryland got started, we need to look across the Atlantic Ocean to the continent of Europe. In the 1400s, 1500s, and 1600s, the countries in Europe were going through big changes. It was a time of many new ideas. Scientists made important discoveries. New inventions like the printing press helped spread knowledge and ideas.

Governments were changing, too. Kings and queens were growing stronger. They wanted to make their nations even more powerful. Countries in Europe began to compete with each other. One way to become more powerful was to become richer. Nations gained wealth by trading goods with people from other continents. Europeans traded lumber, furs, and woolen cloth for Asian spices, jewels, and silks.

European countries sent explorers to search for new trade routes, especially to Asia. When Columbus sailed to islands in what is now called the Caribbean Sea, he thought he had found the East Indies. Soon, however, the Europeans figured out that they had not landed in Asia.

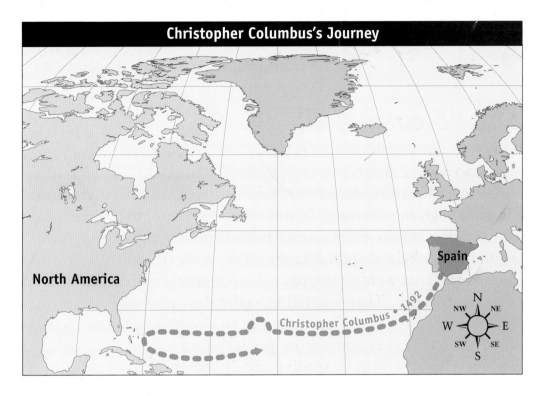

Christopher Columbus's Journey

Spain

North America

Christopher Columbus · 1492

N
NW · NE
W · E
SW · SE
S

Christopher Columbus thought he had found a sea route to the East Indies, islands near Asia. **Where had Columbus actually sailed to?**

The explorers claimed to have discovered a new land. They called it the "New World." As you know, this part of the world was not new to everyone. People had been living here for thousands of years.

Claiming the Land

European kings and queens were excited about the discovery. They wanted to *conquer*, or defeat and take over by force, lands to build their empires. Explorers from Portugal, Spain, Holland, Italy, England, and France sailed to North and South America and claimed land for their rulers. At first, explorers looked for gold. They found some gold and other precious metals in South America. Before long, explorers and traders were sailing up and down the coast of North America. They did not find gold here, but they found timber, furs, and good soil for farming.

Europeans wanted to start colonies on the lands they had claimed. A *colony* is a settlement or land ruled by another country. European countries sent people to start colonies. The colonists were expected to supply raw materials, such as metals, timber, furs, and food for the country they came from. *Raw materials* are used to make other goods.

Who Was First?

Christopher Columbus sailed for the king and queen of Spain in 1492. People today often say that he was the first European to see America. However, we know that sailors from Scandinavia, called Vikings, came to North America long before Columbus. Some historians think that other ships from Europe, Africa, or Asia also sailed to America before Columbus.

Early Colonies

Europeans first settled on islands in what is now known as the Caribbean Sea. Later, they began settling in North and South America. Some early colonies were small and did not survive. People died from *disease*, or sickness, and *starvation*, or a lack of food.

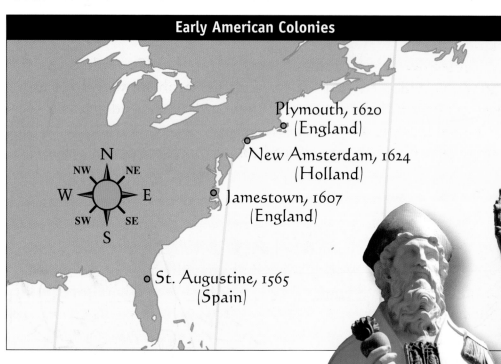

Early American Colonies

Plymouth, 1620
(England)

New Amsterdam, 1624
(Holland)

Jamestown, 1607
(England)

St. Augustine, 1565
(Spain)

Countries in Europe set up colonies in the New World. **What were the names of these early colonies?**

St. Augustine, Florida

The Spanish started the first European colony in North America that survived. It was St. Augustine, in Florida. The Spanish used this colony to guard their ships that sailed along the Atlantic Coast. They also sent the *missionaries* to try to convert the local Indians to the Catholic religion, the religion of the king and queen of Spain. To *convert* means to convince someone to accept a religion. Sometimes missionaries forced Indians to convert.

The colony of St. Augustine was named after a Catholic saint. This is a statue of St. Augustine. **How can you tell from this statue that St. Augustine was a religious man?**

Jamestown, Virginia

The first English colony that survived was Jamestown, in Virginia. It was founded by a group of Englishmen who belonged to the Church of England, the church of the king and queen. The men hoped they would make great wealth for themselves and for England. The king of England gave them the power in Virginia. At first, the leaders of the group made all the rules and laws for the colony. Later, Virginia had a colonial assembly that made laws.

Jamestown had troubles in its early years. The early colonists starved and died from diseases. Another problem was that the wealthy men did not want to do the hard work needed to survive in the wilderness. However, over time, Virginia became an important colony that produced tobacco and other farm products.

Captain John Smith helped establish Jamestown and mapped the Chesapeake Bay.

Colonists began building the Jamestown settlement in Virginia. **What do you think the Indians were thinking as they watched the colonists build buildings and make so many changes to the land?**

Plymouth, Massachusetts

Another early English colony was Plymouth, in Massachusetts. Plymouth was founded by men and women called Pilgrims. They were Christians, but they did not belong to the Church of England. Their religion was not the same as the king and queen's, and they were not treated well in England. They were looking for a place where they would be free to practice their religion.

The Pilgrims set sail for the New World on a ship called the *Mayflower*. While they were still on board the ship, they made an agreement called the Mayflower Compact about the government they would set up. They agreed that they would elect a governor to run the colony. They also agreed that decisions would be made in group meetings, where each man would have a vote.

After the Pilgrims arrived in present-day Massachusetts, the local Indians saved them from starvation by giving them food and teaching them to grow local plants and hunt animals and harvest seafood nearby. Soon, the colonists were able to feed themselves.

According to legend, Pilgrims stepped from the Mayflower *onto Plymouth Rock.* **What year is carved into the rock and why do you think it is an important year to remember?**

Linking the Present to the Past

Today, towns in Massachusetts and other New England states still hold meetings at which people make decisions about matters that affect the town. Men and women, who live in the town, can come to the meetings and vote.

While still on board the Mayflower, *the Pilgrims signed the Mayflower Compact that outlined the type of government they would set up.* **What clues in this picture tell you that the men were on board a ship when they signed this document?**

Americans trace our Thanksgiving holiday back to the time of the first harvest in the Plymouth colony. The Pilgrims shared a meal with the local Indians who had helped them survive. **What do you think the artist wants us to think when we look at this painting?**

① KEY IDEA REVIEW

1. Why did European rulers want to conquer new lands?
2. How did colonists in North America help countries in Europe become more wealthy and powerful?
3. Describe one of the first European colonies in North America.

KEY IDEA

The English were the first to start a colony in Maryland.

WORDS TO UNDERSTAND

charter
consent
contract
freeman
indenture
inherit
proprietor
toleration

Starting the Maryland Colony

George Calvert was a government leader and a friend of King Charles I in England. But after Calvert decided to practice the Catholic religion, he had to give up his job. Catholics were not allowed to vote or hold government jobs in England. King Charles I gave his friend land in America to make up for the lost job. He gave Calvert the official title Lord Baltimore and said he could set up a colony on the land.

Lord Baltimore was called the *proprietor*, or owner, of the colony. He had power in Maryland, just as the king had power in England.

George Calvert died before any colonists came to Maryland. His land and the title Lord Baltimore went to his son Cecilius Calvert. Cecilius's brother, Leonard, came here to be governor of the colony. You will read more about this later in the chapter.

What Do You Think?

Do you think it is fair to make a person give up his or her job because of their religion?

The king of England gave George Calvert land in America to set up the Maryland colony. **Can you spot Queen Henrietta Maria, after whom the colony was named, in this picture?**

Many Europeans set sail from Europe to make the dangerous and difficult journey to America. **What do you think the people on this boat that had set sail from Holland might have been thinking and feeling?**

Reasons the Colonists Came to the Colony

In order to start a successful colony, there had to be plenty of people. Around 150 colonists sailed to Maryland on the first ships from England.

The people knew their journey to America would be difficult and dangerous. The colonists would have to work hard to start a new life in America. They knew they would not have the comforts of home in the American wilderness. Why do you think so many people would leave their homes and their families to come to a strange place they had never seen before?

Colonists had many reasons for leaving England and coming to Maryland. However, they all came with great hope for their life in the New World.

Religious Freedom

People all over Europe—especially Protestants and Catholics—were fighting over religion. These two religious groups had been fighting wars for many years.

In England, the king had made himself head of the Church of England. The Church of England was a Protestant church. Everybody had to pay taxes to support the church. If people did not belong to the Church of England, they were not considered to be loyal to the king. They could not participate in politics. They could not even vote. The Calvert family and other wealthy Catholics did not like living without political rights. They did not like paying taxes to support a church they did not belong to.

George Calvert decided that Maryland would be different. He said Maryland would not have an official church and would not collect taxes to support any religion. Both Catholics and Protestants would be allowed to worship freely here. Both would be allowed to hold government jobs. Some people chose to come to Maryland for religious freedom.

The word "Protestant" comes from the word "protest." People in Europe who protested against certain beliefs and practices of the Catholic Church formed Protestant churches.

This document described how people of different religions would be able to worship freely in Maryland. **What is the title of this document?**

Female prisoners from English prisons were brought to the colonies and sold to male settlers. A man might pay 100 pounds of tobacco for a woman prisoner. **How do you think this woman was feeling about being sold?**

Money Problems

Many Europeans were very poor. Bad weather had ruined many crops, so families had little food. Many people left their farms to move to the cities. But many could not find jobs in the cities, and they could not grow their own food in cities. They did not know how they would survive.

To make things worse, people were put in jail if they could not repay money they owed. Once in jail, it was impossible for them to earn money to pay off the money they owed.

The colonies in America offered a way out of trouble. Wealthy people in America paid the cost of people's trips from Europe to the New World. In exchange, poor people worked off the cost of their trip. They signed a *contract*, or written agreement, called an *indenture*. It stated the number of years of work required for payment, usually 5 to 10. These people were called indentured servants. After their indenture was up, the people were free to look for new jobs.

Opportunities to Get Rich

Not everyone who came to Maryland was poor. Some men had money and wanted to make more. They hoped to own a lot of land in America. Some men who came were younger sons of wealthy men. In England, when a man died, most of his property went to his oldest son. Younger sons usually did not *inherit* their father's land and wealth. Many younger sons came to America to make their fortune here.

The Voyage of the Ark and the Dove

The *Ark* and the *Dove* were the first two ships to bring English colonists to the new colony of Maryland. The two small sailing ships sailed into the Chesapeake Bay after four long months at sea.

The ships stopped first at a small island in the Potomac River. The colonists named it St. Clement's Island. Every man, woman, and child was glad the trip was over. Two storms had terrified them. The winds had blown so hard and the waves had risen so high that all the passengers were afraid the ships would sink. They were afraid of a pirate attack. Twelve people had died of a fever during the trip. Sailing the sea was dangerous.

The trip was also very uncomfortable. A few wealthy gentlemen had cabins, but most of the people slept together on the lower deck. They had no privacy. Their bedding, spread out on the deck floor, was often wet.

The Ark *was the larger boat and the* Dove *was the smaller boat. Most of the passengers sailed on the* Ark, *and supplies were carried on the* Dove. **What do you imagine it was like to sail across the ocean on the** Ark**?**

Passengers on the Ark and the Dove

Most of the passengers on the *Ark* and the *Dove* were Englishmen. Most were poor Protestants, but a few were rich Catholics. Many owed money in England. Very few women and children came. Below is a list of a few of the passengers.

Leonard Calvert

Passenger List

Leonard Calvert was only 23 years old when he was named governor of Maryland and sailed to the new colony.

Thomas Cornwallis was Catholic. He paid his own way. He was given land just for coming. For every servant he brought, Cornwallis was given more land. He got rich quickly this way.

William Browne was only 10 years old. He was an indentured servant of Thomas Cornwallis. He had to work as a servant until he was an adult. After he was free, he became a farmer.

Father Andrew White was a Catholic priest. At the age of 54, he was the oldest passenger. He wrote a book about starting the colony. He worked to convert Indians to Christianity.

Mathias de Sousa was an African. He was an indentured servant who worked for Father White. Later, after he served out his indenture, he earned money by sailing a boat and trading furs with the Indians.

Father Andrew White

"Wee came into Chesapeake Bay, and made sayle to the North for Patoemeck river. . . . It is one of the delightfullest waters I ever saw. . . . And now being in our owne Countrey, wee began to give names to places."

—Father Andrew White

St. Mary's City, the First Town

The people who came on the *Ark* and the *Dove* had to choose a place to live. St. Clement's Island was too small. They picked a place where the Yaocomico (Yow·COM·ih·coh) Indians already had a village. The English gave the Indians cloth, axes, and hoes in exchange for the right to settle on the land. The Yaocomicos had already planned to move their village to another location, so this worked well for everybody.

The Yaocomicos helped the colonists. They let them live in their wigwams. They gave them corn and other foods to eat. They taught them to plant corn, beans, and squash together. They taught them what herbs made good medicines. They showed them where to find oysters and clams.

St. Mary's City

St. Mary's City was built next to an Indian village. **How are the colonists' homes different from the Indians' homes in this drawing?**

Soon the colonists began to set up their village. They put up a palisade and built houses. Most houses had only one room and a dirt floor. Because it was spring, they could also begin farming. They planted fields just outside the village.

The colonists called their town St. Mary's City. It was the colony's first capital.

Artifacts from St. Mary's City

One way we learn about what happened in the past is by studying artifacts. St. Mary's City has many artifacts that were buried under the ground. In recent years, archaeologists have begun to dig up these old treasures. Each one is a clue to what people did, how they lived, and what they cared about. Archaeologists find things like dishes and tools. Archaeologists are scientists who study artifacts to learn about how people lived. They also study the foundations, or bottoms, of buildings to figure out how big the buildings were and what they were made of.

In St. Mary's City, archaeologists found a small piece of a blue-and-white dish. They knew that this small piece was just like dishes that were popular in England. They could draw the rest of the design. You can see the small piece that was found and the drawing of the rest of the dish on the right.

In St. Mary's City, archaeologists also found the foundation of an old church. It was made of brick. The scientists now knew that the colonists made buildings out of brick as well as wood. Archaeologists also found the foundation of a print house. This told the scientists that the people in St. Mary's City could print things—maybe laws or flyers with news of the day.

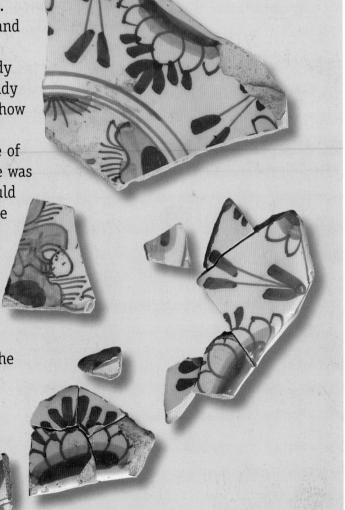

Archaeologists piece together bits of artifacts in order to try to figure out how the people lived. **What artifact are the pieces shown here from?**

The Law of the Land

When the king of England gave George Calvert the land, he also gave him a **charter**. This written contract said exactly what powers the king was giving to the new proprietor.

The Maryland Charter of 1632 was the law of the land. Under the charter, Calvert could give or sell land to colonists. He could collect rent from colonists for their use of the land. He could form an army and fight wars. He could build forts and towns. He could establish courts. He could appoint judges and other government officials. He could make laws for the colony.

The charter also said that there should be an assembly of the freemen. **Freemen** were men who were not indentured or enslaved. The assembly had to **consent**, or agree, to the laws made by the proprietor. This group of men was called the General Assembly. The purpose of the Maryland Charter of 1632 was to establish law and order in Maryland so the colony would succeed.

The Maryland Charter of 1632

The Maryland Charter was the law of the colony. It was important that the laws were written down so everyone could read them. Rulers could not simply make laws whenever they wanted. The colonists lived under the rule of law, not under the power of one person's wishes. The people in the government got their power of authority from written laws. Those laws were meant to limit the power of the government.

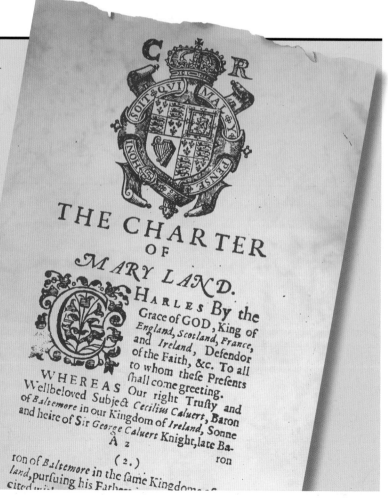

The Maryland Charter outlined the laws of the new colony. The first sentence of the document mentions who the king of England was at this time. **What was his name?**

The General Assembly of Maryland

At first, all the freemen in the colony met together. They discussed issues facing the colony. They could vote on laws issued by the governor. They called this meeting the General Assembly.

Soon, there were so many people in Maryland that it was not practical for them all to meet together. After that, the freemen held elections. The voters chose people to represent them in the General Assembly. This is called representative government. At first, all freemen could vote for members of the General Assembly. Later, only men who owned property could vote for the members.

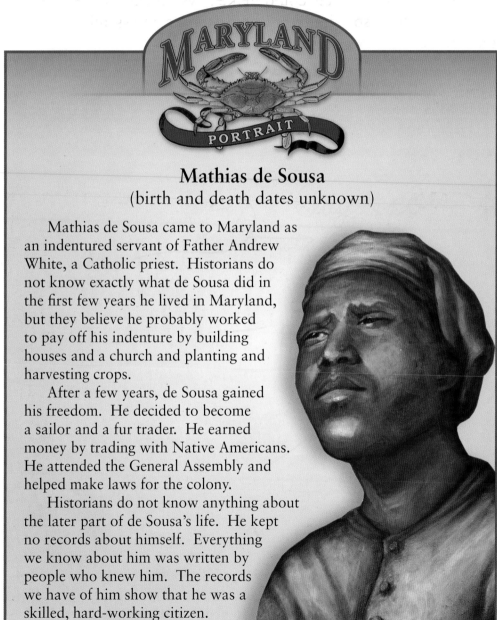

MARYLAND

PORTRAIT

Mathias de Sousa
(birth and death dates unknown)

Mathias de Sousa came to Maryland as an indentured servant of Father Andrew White, a Catholic priest. Historians do not know exactly what de Sousa did in the first few years he lived in Maryland, but they believe he probably worked to pay off his indenture by building houses and a church and planting and harvesting crops.

After a few years, de Sousa gained his freedom. He decided to become a sailor and a fur trader. He earned money by trading with Native Americans. He attended the General Assembly and helped make laws for the colony.

Historians do not know anything about the later part of de Sousa's life. He kept no records about himself. Everything we know about him was written by people who knew him. The records we have of him show that he was a skilled, hard-working citizen.

▶ Illustration by John Vehar

The Toleration Act

The General Assembly gave religious toleration to all Christians. This became known as the Toleration Act. *Toleration* means allowing something without fighting against it. Although the Calverts tolerated people of all religions, this law protected only Christians.

What Do You Think?

The Toleration Act protected only Christians. It did not protect non-Christians. What do you think of a law that protected only Christians?

Leonard Calvert
(1606–1647)

Leonard Calvert was the first governor of Maryland. He was the younger brother of Cecilius Calvert, the proprietor of the colony. Leonard sailed on the *Ark*, with the colony's first settlers. He followed his brother's advice and worked peacefully with the local Indians. He also made sure that the Catholics and Protestants in his group got along with each other. Governor Calvert was in charge of the colony's militia, courts, and finances.

Calvert's wife and two children stayed in England while he lived in Maryland. Calvert visited England several times while he was governor. He served as governor of Maryland until his death.

Challenges in the Maryland Colony

As you read earlier, Cecilius Calvert became the proprietor of Maryland after his father died. Cecilius sent his brother, Leonard, to represent him and named Leonard the governor of the colony. The new government faced several problems.

Problems Over Kent Island

An early challenge to the Calvert family came from William Claiborne, who had come from Virginia. He ran a trading post on Kent Island, near today's Chesapeake Bay Bridge, that did business with local Indians. Claiborne and the Maryland colonists both claimed control of Kent Island. Claiborne led several attacks against Calvert's men. Eventually, Kent Island became part of Maryland.

William Claiborne set up a trading post on Kent Island in the Chesapeake Bay. **Can you describe what is going on in this picture of the trading post?**

Members of the General Assembly met to make laws for the Maryland colony. **What did the mood seem to be at this meeting?**

Problems Making Laws

The Calverts also had some problems making laws for the colony. The charter said the proprietor would make the laws, and the governor would give them to the General Assembly to approve. The men in the General Assembly decided that they should make the laws and then give them to the governor to approve. They wanted the laws to come from the people. At first, the Calverts fought against this, but they finally gave in. From that time on, laws came first from the assembly of the people.

Linking the Present to the Past

The colonial General Assembly worked a lot like our system of government today in Maryland. As in colonial times, today the General Assembly is elected by the people. Today, as in the past, the assembly makes laws, and the governor approves or rejects them.

Problems Over Religion

Another problem the Calverts faced was with the Puritans, a group of Protestants. In England, the Puritans were trying to take over the government. They wanted to get rid of the king and the Church of England. There were Puritans in Maryland and Virginia, too. They decided to try to get rid of the Calvert family. They did not like them because they were loyal to the king. The Puritans also did not like the Calverts because they were Catholic.

Puritans from Virginia attacked Maryland. They forced Governor Leonard Calvert to run away to save his life. The Puritans took control of Maryland and ended the colony's religious toleration. The next year Leonard Calvert gathered soldiers and took back Maryland. He made religious toleration the law again. Leonard Calvert died a year later.

More Fighting Over Religion

There was more fighting over religion in Maryland. Catholics, Puritans, and supporters of the Church of England all wanted to be in control. In the end, the king decided to rule Maryland himself. He appointed governors who were not members of the Calvert family.

Puritans wanted to have power in the Maryland colony. **Why did they want power?**

Chapter 4: Colonial Maryland

Colonists were working hard to establish themselves in the New World. **What information can you gather from this picture about what life was like for white men who owned property?**

The king said the Church of England would be the official church in Maryland. That meant that everyone, no matter what their religion was, had to pay taxes to support that church. Catholics now were not allowed to build churches or worship in public. Only members of the Church of England and other Protestants could vote. Religious freedom ended in Maryland.

After some years, some Calvert family members joined the Church of England. Then members of the family could serve as governors of Maryland again.

Voting in the Colony

When the Calverts regained their power, not all of the freemen in the colony were allowed to vote. A person had to be male and own property in order to vote. Only Protestants could vote. Catholics could not vote. Jews could not vote. Colonial Maryland never did stop people from voting because of the color of their skin. However, only a few blacks owned enough property to vote.

② KEY IDEA REVIEW

1. Explain the events that led to Leonard Calvert becoming the first governor of the Maryland colony.
2. Why did people from Europe come to the Maryland colony?
3. List two things the Maryland Charter of 1632 said.
4. Tell about one of the challenges in the Maryland colony.

KEY IDEA

Despite problems, many people from different cultures helped the Maryland colony grow.

WORDS TO UNDERSTAND

custom
enslave
frontier
gentry
immune
plantation
tutor

Some colonists in Maryland grew tobacco. **What work are the people in this picture doing?**

More Colonists Arrive

Soon other colonists joined the first groups in Maryland. They brought more indentured servants. The colony needed many workers to help clear land, plant crops, and build houses. Women began to join the men here. Maryland became home to many families. People quickly settled land all along both sides of the Chesapeake Bay.

Farming and Trade

All the new people changed the natural environment. The colonists cut down many forests for farms and towns. In later years, they drained wetlands, so they could also use that land.

People grew and raised their own food. They grew corn and vegetables. Some people brought seeds with them from England. The first colonists got farm animals from Virginia. They raised cows and hogs. The colonists grew tobacco and sold the leaves to buyers in England. Tobacco wore out the soil. After four years or so, farmers had to plant tobacco in new fields.

Colonial Money System

When colonists arrived in Maryland, they brought Britain's money system with them. Colonists used British money to pay for most goods. Sometimes they used tobacco or other agricultural products to trade for goods.

Farmers hauled their tobacco to ships that carried it to other colonies and to Europe to be sold. **Why do you think farmers lived near rivers and the Chesapeake Bay?**

Farmers spread out along the rivers, where ships could come pick up their crops. Tobacco and other crops were hard to carry very far across the land. There were no real roads. The same ships that picked up the tobacco and other crops from the farmers brought goods from England, such as cloth, tools, and other things that were not available here. Trading goods was an important way to make money.

As the colony grew, some men became very wealthy. The men who owned the best land along the rivers had the money to bring over a lot of indentured servants to work for them. More workers could grow more tobacco. With the money the landowners got from selling their tobacco, they could buy more land. This land was the reason for their wealth and power.

Lesson 3: The Maryland Colony Grows

Indians and Colonists

Native Americans and colonists learned from each other and often shared knowledge. However, there were also problems. Many Indians died from illnesses Europeans brought with them to the New World. Many Indians were not happy about the growing colony. Woodland tribes that had been living here for a long time wanted to keep their lands, traditions, and culture.

Learning and Sharing

As the peoples of Europe and America came together, they shared their cultures and ideas. The European colonists learned a lot from the Native Americans. The Indians taught colonists how to grow corn, beans, and squash. They taught them where there was good fishing and hunting. They showed them the routes through the forests. They taught them about the local climate.

The Indians in both Maryland and Virginia also grew tobacco. They used it only during special ceremonies. Tobacco became an important crop for the colonists and a major source of their wealth. Colonists called it "the stinking weed."

The colonists helped the Native Americans as well by trading with them. Colonists had strong metal tools and pots and pans. They had sharp metal knives. They had cloth to make clothing. The Europeans knew how to make wheels, which the local people did not have. Europeans brought horses, cattle, sheep, and other animals to America.

The colonists and Indians often met to trade. **What were the colonists and Indians trading in this picture?**

Many Indians became sick or even died when the Europeans first came here.
Can you describe what is shown in this picture?

Diseases

Unfortunately, not everything the colonists and Indians traded was good. Europeans brought diseases like smallpox and measles with them when they crossed the Atlantic. These diseases had not existed in America. Indians were not immune to the diseases, and they became very sick. To be *immune* to a disease means to have a resistance to getting it. Sometimes whole villages died. These diseases weakened Indian tribes and made it more difficult to keep the Europeans from taking their land.

Problems Over Land

The colonists wanted as much land as they could get. Sometimes they bought the land from the Indians. Other times they took land by tricking the Indians or fighting against them.

As the colonists took over more land and changed the environment, Indians could not live as they had before. There were fewer animals to hunt. There was less land for planting crops. The Indians could no longer meet all their own needs. They began to rely on the trade items they got from the colonists.

After some years, the colonists claimed they owned all the land. They forced Indians to move onto small pieces of land. Many Piscataways and Nanticokes who survived moved away from the colonists. Soon, most Indians left Maryland. Only a few remained in their traditional homes.

Slaves were sold at auctions to the highest bidders. **What emotions do you think this enslaved man being auctioned was feeling?**

Africans in Early Maryland

A few years after St. Mary's City was founded, a ship carrying 13 Africans arrived. Other ships carrying more Africans followed. Some Africans came with indenture contracts and became free after their debt was paid. But others were captured and *enslaved* and brought to Maryland.

Some years later, Maryland passed a law saying that Africans without indenture contracts would be slaves for life. The law also said the children of slaves would be enslaved for life.

Slavery was a very cruel system. Human beings were treated as property. Slaves had to work their whole lives without any pay. They were often treated badly.

Contributions of Africans

Many African slaves in Maryland grew and harvested tobacco, which brought great wealth to large landowners. All the colonies benefited from the hard work of enslaved men, women, and children.

Africans brought a lot of knowledge about farming with them to America. They grew crops, such as yams, that were native to Africa. Africans also brought knowledge about many crafts. Some Africans were good metal, leather, and woodworkers. Others could sew clothing.

Blending of Cultures

Gradually African culture began to blend with European culture. While Africans had their own religions and **customs**, or ways of doing things, they also learned about other religions and customs from the colonists. When Africans first arrived here, many could not speak English. Over time, people learned English, and their children grew up speaking English.

During these early years, some Africans and whites married. Later, there were laws against this. Both Africans and whites married Indians. Many African Americans and whites today have Indian ancestors.

Africans and Indians shared their knowledge and traditions. Some Africans who married Native Americans went to live in Indian settlements. Some slaves who ran away also went to Native American areas.

Parts of African culture gradually became part of the wider American culture. For example, many American forms of music, such as jazz and the blues, came from African music.

Africans brought the banjo with them to the New World. **Have you ever heard someone play the banjo?**

Africans brought their culture to the New World. **What parts of African culture are shown in this drawing?**

Everyday Life in Colonial Maryland

There were many different groups of people living in colonial Maryland. Let's learn about the people who lived here around 1750.

Gentry

Rich families were called the *gentry*. Many owned *plantations*, or large farms. Some men had other businesses or were lawyers. Other men held high government positions. Women were in charge of home life. They ran the house and took care of the children.

Children of the gentry were educated. Often a *tutor* came to the house to teach the lessons. Both boys and girls learned to read and write. Boys studied Latin and Greek. Some boys traveled to Europe for more education. Girls learned to sew and do needlework. Both boys and girls learned to play a musical instrument.

The gentry lived in large brick homes. They bought furniture that had been shipped to the colony from England. They owned books, musical instruments, gold jewelry, and fine clothes. Most families owned slaves and had servants.

Families in the Middle

Many families were neither rich nor poor. They owned a home and some land. Some rented land because they could not afford to buy it. Some were merchants, who sold goods to people in towns. Many worked at crafts. For example, they were carpenters or cobblers (shoemakers). Many families had homes with just one or two rooms. Most of their furniture and clothing was made in Maryland. Their clothes were often made from English cloth.

Families in the middle worked very hard. Men worked in the fields and at their craft. Women made clothing, prepared meals, took care of the garden, and made household items. Most families had at least one slave or servant. Some had several.

Both boys and girls helped with the family's work. Some children, mostly boys, went to school.

In colonial society, members of the gentry were the wealthiest. **What evidence do you see in this picture that suggests that this child had special advantages?**

Hired Workers and Servants

Men and women who could not afford to buy or rent land worked for other people. Many worked on farms or in the homes of wealthier families. Some helped craftsmen like shoemakers. Hired workers hoped to save enough money to buy land someday. They lived in small houses. They made their own furniture.

You have read about indentured servants. These men, women, and children had to work for a certain number of years to pay for their trip to Maryland. During that time, they were not paid for their work and they were not free to take another job. After they worked off their indenture, these people became free. Many of them then became hired workers.

Slaves and Free Blacks

Over the years, there were fewer indentured servants and more slaves working in Maryland. By the mid-1700s, slaves did most of the work growing tobacco. Some worked in homes doing cooking and cleaning or taking care of children. Some learned skilled crafts like carpentry.

Slaves often lived in small cabins with homemade furniture. Most had family members who lived on the same plantation or nearby. However, there were no laws that kept slave owners from selling a slave to someone who lived far away.

Some African American families had been free since the earliest colonial days. Some became free later. Many free blacks were hired workers. Some owned small farms. Children often worked along with their parents. Some children learned to read and write, although they did not go to school.

Free blacks had more rights than enslaved people, but they did not have all the rights that white people enjoyed.

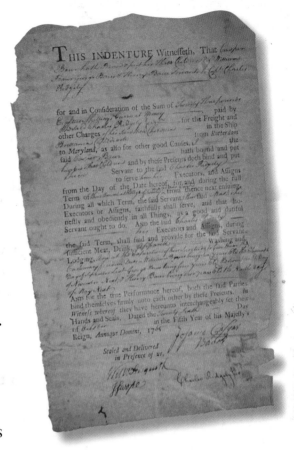

People who could not pay for their trip to the Maryland colony often came as indentured servants. They signed a paper like this one. This indenture was an agreement about how many years they would work without pay before they became free. **Why do you think some of this paper is in cursive writing and some is not?**

MARYLAND SOCIAL STUDIES SKILLS AND PROCESSES SKILLS

Compare Two Cultures Using a Venn Diagram
Copy this Venn diagram onto your own piece of paper. Compare the lives of servants to slaves. In what ways were their lives similar? In what ways were their lives different?

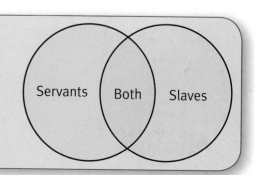

Servants | Both | Slaves

Colonial Towns in Maryland

At first, most people did not settle in towns. They spread out on farms across the Maryland colony. Small towns began to grow as more people moved to the colony and businesses grew.

Annapolis and Other Early Towns

As more people settled in central Maryland, the capital was moved from St. Mary's City to Annapolis. Soon, Annapolis was the colony's largest town. The General Assembly met there. Lawyers and merchants lived there. Annapolis had inns for all its visitors. Men and women ran shops that sold food, paper goods, cloth, hats, shoes, boots, furniture, candles, clocks, silver dishes, and jewelry.

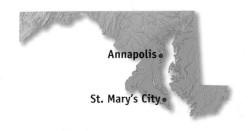

Annapolis grew to be the Maryland colony's largest town. **What evidence do you see in this picture that many people lived in Annapolis?**

King William's School

The first public school in Maryland was King William's School in Annapolis. This school was not like public schools today. It was for white boys only. Students learned Greek, Latin, writing, and other subjects to prepare them for the new William and Mary College in Virginia.

The colony's first newspaper, the *Maryland Gazette*, was published in Annapolis. Jonas Green was a well-known publisher of this paper. When he died, his wife, Anne Catharine Green, took over.

Other early towns were Oxford, Chestertown, Joppa, Port Tobacco, and Baltimore. All these towns were built near rivers and the bay. Ships from all the colonies and from England came to ports in the Chesapeake region. Men opened shipyards to build and repair boats. Port cities were busy places.

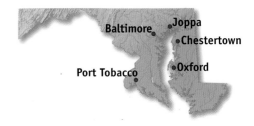

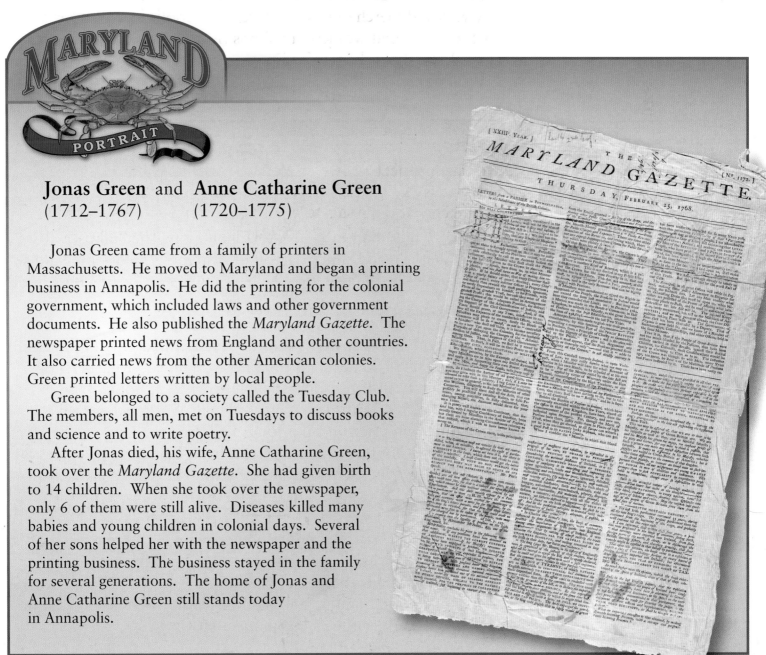

Jonas Green and Anne Catharine Green
(1712–1767)   (1720–1775)

Jonas Green came from a family of printers in Massachusetts. He moved to Maryland and began a printing business in Annapolis. He did the printing for the colonial government, which included laws and other government documents. He also published the *Maryland Gazette*. The newspaper printed news from England and other countries. It also carried news from the other American colonies. Green printed letters written by local people.

Green belonged to a society called the Tuesday Club. The members, all men, met on Tuesdays to discuss books and science and to write poetry.

After Jonas died, his wife, Anne Catharine Green, took over the *Maryland Gazette*. She had given birth to 14 children. When she took over the newspaper, only 6 of them were still alive. Diseases killed many babies and young children in colonial days. Several of her sons helped her with the newspaper and the printing business. The business stayed in the family for several generations. The home of Jonas and Anne Catharine Green still stands today in Annapolis.

Men from the county met to gather information to lay out the new town of Baltimore. **What types of planning do you think the men were doing?**

Baltimore Town

At first, Baltimore was just farmland along the Patapsco River. Then, Charles and Daniel Carroll of Annapolis sold some land so a town could be built on it. The new town was located on a good harbor. Roads were planned. The land was split into lots for people to buy.

Baltimore grew slowly. After 20 years, it had only 25 houses, 2 taverns (bars), 1 church, 1 tobacco warehouse, 1 barbershop, and 1 insurance office. Craftspeople worked at home.

By the 1750s, Baltimore was growing. Workers built mills along the town's streams, the Jones Falls and the Gwynns Falls. Ships carried flour, wheat, and bread from Baltimore to places far away to sell. Iron was found near Baltimore. Some of this iron was shipped to England. Local farmers grew tobacco that was also sold to England.

By the late 1700s, Baltimore had grown into a large town. Big ships came to its harbor, bringing goods from England and other colonies. The ships took local products with them when they sailed away. Shipbuilding and manufacturing were important in Baltimore. The town was becoming a city.

Chapter 4: Colonial Maryland

Maryland's Frontier

Eventually, colonists spread out to the frontier hills and valleys in central and Western Maryland. The *frontier* was unsettled land covered with forests before the colonists came.

People living on the frontier grew vegetables, fruits, and wheat. Wheat was very important in the colony. Most families that grew wheat lived on small farms and did most of the work themselves. They usually did not have slaves or indentured servants. Some of these farmers were Germans. They were hard workers. At home, they spoke German. Their children and grandchildren, who were born here, spoke English.

Many towns, such as Baltimore and Chestertown, became centers for shipping wheat to other colonies. These towns also shipped wheat to the West Indies. The people who built and owned the sailing ships that carried wheat made good money.

Much of the wheat was ground into flour before it was shipped. Towns developed along the fall line, where there was rushing water to power the mills.

Wheat farmers needed towns as central places to sell or ship wheat. They also needed mills to grind their wheat into flour. They needed stores where they could buy supplies that were sent from the East. Towns grew to meet the need for mills and stores.

The colonists settled the lands of central and Western Maryland. People living on the frontier grew their own crops. **What crops did the colonists in this picture grow?**

Frontier Towns

One important town on the frontier was Frederick. A man named Daniel Dulany had bought a lot of land in western Maryland. He wanted to sell the land, so he built a town to attract farmers. Dulany offered land at a good price to craftsmen and shopkeepers who moved there. The farmers followed. Frederick became the center of Maryland's frontier.

Jonathan Hager was inspired by the success of Frederick. Thirty miles farther west, Hager laid out a town on land that he owned. Hager wanted to name his town after his wife Elizabeth, but people called it Hager's Town. The name stuck.

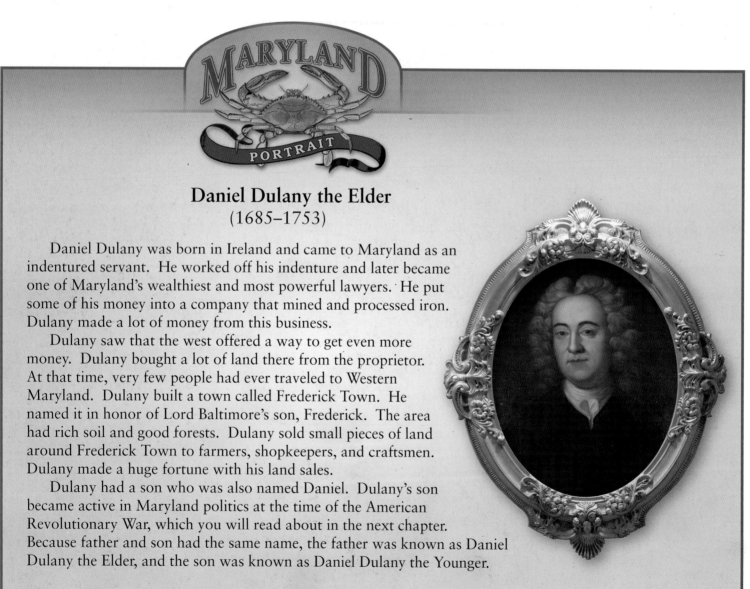

Daniel Dulany the Elder
(1685–1753)

Daniel Dulany was born in Ireland and came to Maryland as an indentured servant. He worked off his indenture and later became one of Maryland's wealthiest and most powerful lawyers. He put some of his money into a company that mined and processed iron. Dulany made a lot of money from this business.

Dulany saw that the west offered a way to get even more money. Dulany bought a lot of land there from the proprietor. At that time, very few people had ever traveled to Western Maryland. Dulany built a town called Frederick Town. He named it in honor of Lord Baltimore's son, Frederick. The area had rich soil and good forests. Dulany sold small pieces of land around Frederick Town to farmers, shopkeepers, and craftsmen. Dulany made a huge fortune with his land sales.

Dulany had a son who was also named Daniel. Dulany's son became active in Maryland politics at the time of the American Revolutionary War, which you will read about in the next chapter. Because father and son had the same name, the father was known as Daniel Dulany the Elder, and the son was known as Daniel Dulany the Younger.

During the French and Indian War, fighting took place along the frontier. **Can you describe the conditions that these soldiers fought under?**

French and Indian War

France controlled a lot of the land around the 13 British colonies. Both Britain and France wanted their empires to grow. They fought over the land in America. The Indians also wanted the land. It was their home and hunting grounds.

When the British colonists came, they cut down the forests to build farms. When the French came, they did not disturb the forests. The French wanted the Indians to be able to hunt because then they could get furs from the Indians. The French and the Indians traded with each other. The Indians gave the French furs in exchange for metal knives, guns, and pots.

Britain used men from the 13 colonies to fight against the French. Soldiers defended western settlements like Frederick and Hagerstown. Some people fled from Western Maryland to Baltimore. The colonists called this the French and Indian War because they were fighting against both the French and Indians.

Three countries had been united by England. They were England, Scotland, and Wales. Together, they are called Great Britain.

Results of the War

After seven years, Britain won the war and control of land all the way west to the Mississippi River and in Canada. American men had gained military experience. They had practiced fighting in colonial *militias*, or armies made up of citizens with some military training. Men like George Washington had learned to lead troops. Colonial assemblies had helped the people organize and pay for some of the costs of the war.

The colonists became more and more upset as British soldiers tried to enforce new policies and taxes. **Can you pick out which men are the soldiers and which are the colonists in this picture?**

When colonists bought playing cards, they had to pay the stamp tax. **Do these cards look like the cards people play with today?**

More Signs of Trouble

Even though the British had gained control of western lands, they did not want to fight any more wars against Indians. Wars were difficult to fight and cost a lot of money. The British told the colonists not to move west of the Appalachian Mountains, where many Indians lived. But some colonists had already bought land there. They wanted to live on the land. Others wanted to sell the land they had bought to other Americans who might settle there.

The British also wanted the colonists to pay for the war. It had cost a lot of money. The British began to ask Americans to pay new taxes. The British would use the money from the taxes to pay off the war *debt*, or money that was owed.

The colonists believed they had already paid. They had fought on the side of the British, and they had given Britain supplies during the French and Indian War.

The Stamp Act

The Stamp Act was one British law that made the colonists pay a new tax. The colonists had to buy stamps to put on all kinds of papers, such as business and legal papers, marriage licenses, newspapers, and even playing cards. If they did not have stamps, the documents were not legal, and the newspapers could not be sold.

Chapter 5: Revolution and a New Nation

An Annapolis merchant named Zachariah Hood, who was in Britain at the time, took the job of stamp tax collector for Maryland. When he returned to Maryland, a mob tore down his warehouse where the stamps were stored. Hood fled to New York.

Maryland's General Assembly met to discuss the Stamp Act. The men agreed that Britain did not have the right to tax the colonists. The colonists were not allowed to send representatives to Parliament (the group that made laws in London). A *representative* is a person elected to speak, vote, or act for other people. Because they were not represented, many colonists thought Parliament should not be allowed to tax them. They said that only the colonial assembly, which was elected by Marylanders, could tax them.

The rallying cry became "No taxation without representation!" Some men formed a group to *protest*, or speak out against, the taxes. The group was called the Sons of Liberty.

The colonists protested so much that the British *repealed*, or took away, the Stamp Act. The colonists learned important lessons from this. They also learned how to organize and protest.

The Sons of Liberty

Up and down the colonies, men joined together to form the Sons of Liberty to fight the Stamp Act and other British policies they thought were hurting them. Members included merchants, shopkeepers, and craftsmen. William Lux organized a Sons of Liberty group in Baltimore. Samuel Chase, William Paca, and others organized a group in Annapolis.

The Sons of Liberty worked together to force the British to repeal the Stamp Act. After the British repealed the Stamp Act, protests died down for a few years.

The Sons of Liberty protested what they believed was Britain's unfair treatment of the colonists. **What do you think the man in the blue jacket is saying to the other colonists at this meeting?**

The Tea Act

The British did not give up on taxing the colonists. Next, they placed a tax on tea. The British said that tea had to be shipped to America on British ships and not on ships from other countries. The British also tried to force the colonists to buy tea from the British East India Company. Once again, the colonists resisted.

The Boston Tea Party

The colonists' first protest was in Boston, Massachusetts. Men disguised as Indians went down to the harbor. To *disguise* means to change the appearance of something. The men went on board a British ship and dumped all the tea into the water. Robert Sessions, a man who took part, described what happened:

> *The chests were . . . opened, the tea emptied over the side, and the chests thrown overboard. . . . Although there were many people on the wharf, [there was] entire silence.*

This event was called the Boston Tea Party. British leaders were angry with the colonists over the Boston Tea Party. They said Boston's harbor would be closed until the colonists paid for the ruined tea. This made the colonists mad.

In many towns throughout the colonies, women organized the Daughters of Liberty. They **boycotted**, or refused to buy, tea. They shared recipes for other drinks. The women's boycott hurt the British East India Company and also British ship owners.

During the Boston Tea Party, colonists dressed as Indians raided a British ship that carried tea. **Where did the men dump the tea?**

When a ship named the Peggy Stewart *arrived in Annapolis carrying tea, some Marylanders were very angry. To protect himself and his family from harm, the ship's owner burned his own ship.* **What are the people in the smaller boat doing?**

Other Complaints

The colonists had other complaints about the British. In Maryland, some colonists who were not members of the Church of England complained about having to pay taxes that were used to support the church. Everyone's tax money went to support that one church. Catholics, Presbyterians, Lutherans, Quakers, and Jews had to pay the tax. Many people did not think it was fair.

Marylanders were also upset about a law that kept many people from being free to practice their own religion. The Calvert family, who were Catholics, had founded the colony. However, now all the top colonial officials were members of the Church of England. Catholics were not allowed to worship in churches, only in private homes. Catholics and people who practiced some other religions could not vote or hold any government office. They did not like this.

Different colonies had different problems with the British. Colonists everywhere grew more and more angry. They did not want to take orders from rulers who lived on the other side of the Atlantic Ocean, over 3,000 miles away.

Delegates held a meeting called the First Continental Congress to discuss the problems the colonists had with the British. **What do you think these men were thinking and feeling as they left the meeting?**

The First Continental Congress

Men, called delegates, from all across the colonies met in Philadelphia, Pennsylvania, to talk about their problems with the British. A *delegate* is a person elected to represent and act for another. This meeting was called the First Continental Congress. The delegates said the laws and taxes were hurting the colonies. They said they did not have to obey British laws that hurt them. They said colonists should have more rights. They agreed to stop trading with Britain until they could get what they wanted. The delegates began to work together. They encouraged all of the colonists to *unite*, or come together, against the British.

The Maryland Convention

At home, delegates from all across Maryland met in Annapolis. They called this meeting the Maryland Convention. The delegates were popular leaders who believed British laws were unfair. Even though it was illegal, the delegates began to make laws for Maryland at the convention. Soon, the convention became the government of Maryland. It took the place of the old colonial government. The colonists believed they had the right to set up a new government because the old one had been unfair. The change in government was peaceful. The colonial governor did not fight back. He simply left Maryland and went home to Britain.

Governor Robert Eden was the last British colonial governor.

The Colonists Get Ready to Fight

The colonists were still angry that the British had closed Boston's harbor after the Boston Tea Party. Merchants who shipped things out of Boston could no longer earn money. Nothing could be shipped into Boston, either. Massachusetts bought a lot of food from colonies farther south. The Maryland Convention voted to send help. Maryland joined other colonies in sending supplies to the people in Boston.

In Maryland, Virginia, and other colonies, British rules were hurting the tobacco trade. Planters were just as angry as the townspeople of Boston were.

Colonists were also angry because the British told some of the colonial assemblies that they could no longer meet. Many colonists began to believe it would take a fight to bring about change. They started to collect guns, cannons, and *ammunition*, including bullets and cannon balls, to get ready for fighting if it broke out. At the same time, Britain was sending more soldiers and ships to America to try to control the colonists.

Colonists became angrier and angrier over British rule. **What clues in this picture suggest that these colonists were upset?**

❶ KEY IDEA REVIEW

1. Why did the British ask the colonists to pay new taxes they had never paid before?
2. How did the colonists react after the British closed Boston's harbor?
3. Write one thing that happened at the First Continental Congress.

125

KEY IDEA

The 13 colonies united to fight for their independence from Britain.

WORDS TO UNDERSTAND

armed
declare
independence
privateer
sacrifice
surrender

The Revolution Begins

A British general sent troops to take away the weapons and ammunition that colonists in Massachusetts had collected. The colonists had stored the supplies in a town called Concord, near Boston. When the British reached Lexington, on the way to Concord, they were met by armed men from the local militia. To be *armed* means to have weapons. The British and the colonial militia fired shots at one another in Lexington. Then, there was more shooting in Concord and later on the road back to Boston. Men on both sides were killed. This was the beginning of the American Revolutionary War. The revolution is also called by other names, including the American Revolution and the War for Independence. *Independence* means not being under the control of others.

Colonists and British soldiers met at Concord Bridge. Americans called the British soldiers "Redcoats" or "Lobster-Backs." **Why do you think they chose those nicknames?**

Patriots and Loyalists

The American colonists were divided. About one-third wanted independence and were willing to fight for it. About one third wanted to stay under the rule of the British king and did not want a war. The last third did not care much one way or the other.

The colonists who believed they should break away from Great Britain and start a new country were called Patriots. The colonists who were loyal to Great Britain were called Loyalists.

Participate in a Class Debate

If you were one of the colonists, would you choose to be a Loyalist or a Patriot? Your teacher will divide your class into two groups. One group will be Loyalists. The other group will be Patriots. Your group should discuss these questions:

- Were you born in Great Britain or in America?
- Do you still have relatives in Britain?
- How have Britain's rules and taxes affected you?
- How has trade with Britain benefitted you?
- What is your religion?
- What will happen if Britain wins the war?
- What will happen if America wins the war?
- Do you believe people should have the right to choose their own leaders?
- What should people do if they disagree with a law?
- Is America so far away from Britain that it should be a separate country?

Second Continental Congress

Once the fighting began, more Americans demanded independence. They wanted to rule themselves. A Second Continental Congress met in Philadelphia. The delegates created a Continental Army, with George Washington as the commander.

America Declares Independence

About a year later, the delegates agreed to *declare*, or announce, independence from Britain. Thomas Jefferson of Virginia and several other men decided on the exact words to use to explain what they were doing and why they were doing it. On July 4, 1776, the delegates approved the Declaration of Independence.

The men who voted for independence committed a crime. They plotted, or acted, against the government. The punishment for treason was death. What the signers did was very risky and very brave. The men believed what they did was right.

The delegates signed the Declaration of Independence, which said that the colonies were free from British rule. **What do you think the feeling in the room was as these men signed the document?**

Marylanders and the Declaration of Independence

Maryland was slower than the other colonies to agree to fight for independence. Many Marylanders hoped to be able to get along with Britain. Many of the delegates from the other colonies at the Continental Congress in Philadelphia were unhappy that Maryland was not supporting independence.

Finally, Maryland leaders like Samuel Chase and Charles Carroll agreed that Maryland had to join the other colonies in declaring independence. They said Maryland could not be the only colony not to join the others. They urged all Marylanders to support this decision. The Maryland Convention finally authorized Maryland delegates in Philadelphia to vote for independence. Marylanders had thought long and hard before taking such a serious step.

Today, you can take a trip to the National Archives in Washington, D.C., to see the Declaration of Independence. **Why do you think this document is stored in a glass case?**

What Do You Think ?

Why do you think the signers of the Declaration of Independence were willing to sacrifice everything they had for independence? Would you have been willing to **sacrifice**, or give up, so much?

The Declaration of Independence

When in the course of human events, it becomes necessary for one people to dissolve the political bonds which have connected them with another . . . they should declare the causes which impel them to the separation.

We hold these truths to be self-evident: That all men are created equal; that they are endowed by their creator with certain unalienable rights; that among these are life, liberty, and the pursuit of happiness; that to secure these rights, governments are instituted among men, deriving their just powers from the consent of the governed; that whenever any form of government becomes destructive of these ends, it is the right of the people to alter or to abolish it.

The purpose of the Declaration of Independence was to declare the colonies independent from the rule of Great Britain. Read the headings on the Declaration of Independence and look up words that you do not understand. **What does "unanimous declaration" mean?**

The words above begin one of the most famous documents in the history of the world. Because the Declaration of Independence was written over 200 years ago, the language is a little hard to understand. Here is the meaning:

The first part of the Declaration of Independence says that the writers are going to explain why the colonies are declaring independence from British rule. The colonists felt that they were taking such an important step that they should tell everyone why they were doing it.

The second part begins the explanation. It says that all men are born with certain rights. These rights include life, liberty, and the pursuit of happiness (opportunity to try to find happiness). Governments are supposed to protect these rights. If a government does not protect the rights of the people, then the people can get rid of that government and start a new one.

The Declaration of Independence also says that all governments get their power from the people. That is why the people can and should change their government if it is hurting them.

Next, the Declaration of Independence lists the ways in which the British government had been hurting the colonists. In all, the Declaration of Independence lists 27 ways.

At the end of the list, Jefferson wrote that all these things gave the colonists the right to go to war to fight for independence. It was right because the British had harmed, not protected, the colonists.

Chapter 5: Revolution and a New Nation

Marylanders Sign the Declaration of Independence

In August, a month after the Second Continental Congress agreed to declare independence, the official copy of the Declaration of Independence was signed in Philadelphia. Four men, who were Maryland's delegates at the time, signed for our state.

Thomas Stone
1743–1787
Thomas Stone grew up in Charles County. He rode a horse 10 miles every day to school. He later became a lawyer. Stone worked hard to take care of his wife, three children, and his four younger brothers after the death of his father. Stone was chosen as a delegate to the Maryland Convention in Annapolis and the Second Continental Congress. After independence, he served in the Maryland General Assembly.

William Paca
1740–1799
William Paca grew up in Harford County. He became a lawyer. He helped organize the Sons of Liberty that protested British taxes. He was a member of the Maryland Convention and a delegate to the Second Continental Congress. After independence, he served in the Maryland General Assembly and as a judge. He was elected governor of Maryland three times. He helped found Washington College in Chestertown.

Charles Carroll
1737–1832
Charles Carroll was born into a rich family in Annapolis. He became a lawyer. He led protests before the Revolution. The Maryland Convention chose him as a Maryland delegate to the Second Continental Congress. He was the only signer of the Declaration of Independence who was a Catholic. He later served in the Maryland State Senate and the U.S. Senate. He was a founder of the Baltimore and Ohio Railroad.

Samuel Chase
1743–1811
Samuel Chase was born in Somerset County. Though his father did not have much money, he paid for Chase to get a good education. Chase became a lawyer. He protested British taxes and was a founder of the Annapolis Sons of Liberty. He was called "the Stormy Patriot." Chase was chosen as a delegate to the Second Continental Congress, helped write Maryland's first state constitution, and served as a judge in Maryland. He became a judge on the U.S. Supreme Court.

At an important point in the Revolution, George Washington led troops across the Delaware River to New Jersey. This action took the British troops by surprise. **How did the troops get across the river?**

The American Revolutionary War

General George Washington led the Continental Army. He was a strong leader and a good commander.

Maryland was lucky that no major battles were fought here. There was a lot of action, however, on the Chesapeake Bay. Both the Americans and the British sent ships there. When the armies left the ships to march across the land, they often stole from local farms to get food and firewood.

Marylanders in the Revolution

Many Marylanders left their families and jobs to join the Continental Army. Maryland soldiers were some of the best George Washington had. They fought in New York, New Jersey, Pennsylvania, Virginia, North Carolina, and South Carolina. They made great sacrifices to fight for independence. They risked their lives. Sometimes they did not have uniforms or enough ammunition. Sometimes they were not paid because the government ran out of money.

Maryland's government chose the leaders of our state's army units. Usually they were from the gentry. Farmers, craftsmen, and merchants fought as soldiers.

Some ship captains from Maryland became *privateers*. They attacked and captured enemy ships. They also took the goods from British ships. They got to keep what they captured. Some privateers became quite rich this way.

African Americans, both slave and free, fought in the war, too. Black men who knew the bay piloted ships that patrolled the Chesapeake. Their skill and knowledge of the bay helped to win the war.

German settlers also fought. German farmers from western Maryland and craftsmen and workers from Baltimore formed army units. They fought along with their English-speaking neighbors. For the first time, the Germans were considered to be Americans.

"The Breadbasket of the Revolution"

Maryland's wheat fed many soldiers and sailors. The trade in grain brought a lot of business to Maryland merchants and ship owners. The port of Baltimore grew during the war.

Other products from Maryland were also used in the war. Maryland's factories made cannons. Shipyards built many of the ships used by the American navy.

Some colonial soldiers lived in buildings called barracks, such as these in Frederick. Others had to camp out where they were fighting. **If you had been a soldier during this time, would you have rather lived in barracks or in a tent?**

Slaves in the Revolution

When the Revolution began, the British governor in Virginia, Lord Dunmore, said all slaves who fought on the British side would be free when the war ended. Many slaves from Southern Maryland went to Virginia to join Dunmore's forces. Though the British lost the war, they kept their promise. They sent many slaves to Canada and the West Indies, which were still owned by Britain, where they became free. Many slaves who fought on the American side also became free because of their service.

James Armistead was an assistant to the French general Lafayette, who was fighting with the Americans. Armistead also spied for the Americans. At the end of the war, Armistead became free. He changed his name to James Armistead Lafayette.

James Armistead Lafayette

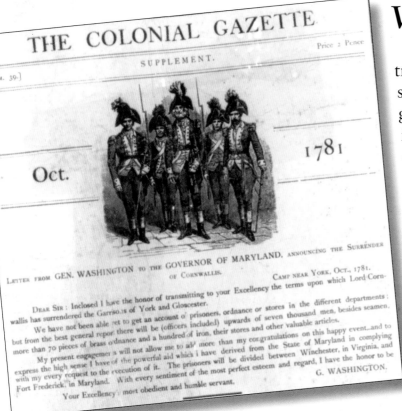

THE COLONIAL GAZETTE

SUPPLEMENT.

Price : Pence

Oct.   1781

LETTER FROM GEN. WASHINGTON TO THE GOVERNOR OF MARYLAND, ANNOUNCING THE SURRENDER OF CORNWALLIS.

CAMP NEAR YORK, OCT., 1781.

DEAR SIR : Inclosed I have the honor of transmitting to your Excellency the terms upon which Lord Cornwallis has surrendered the Garrisons of York and Gloucester.

We have not been able yet to get an account of prisoners, ordnance or stores in the different departments ;
but from the best general report there will be (officers included) upwards of seven thousand men, besides seamen,
more than 70 pieces of brass ordnance and a hundred of iron, their stores and other valuable articles.

My present engagements will not allow me to add more than my congratulations on this happy event—and to
express the high sense I have of the powerful aid which I have derived from the State of Maryland in complying
with my every request to the execution of it. The prisoners will be divided between Winchester, in Virginia, and
Fort Frederick, in Maryland. With every sentiment of the most perfect esteem and regard, I have the honor to be
Your Excellency : most obedient and humble servant.

G. WASHINGTON.

Victory at Last!

After a few years of fighting, the colonial troops needed help to defeat the British. They signed an agreement with France. The French government was happy to help the colonists fight the British. Since the British were their enemies, the French sent supplies and soldiers to help the colonists. The French general Marquis de Lafayette was very popular in America, especially in Maryland. He visited Maryland many times.

The last battle took place at Yorktown, Virginia. American troops, including men from Maryland, defeated the British. The British general Charles Cornwallis ordered his men to *surrender*, or give up fighting.

The Americans had won the Revolution. Now they really would be independent.

The Colonial Gazette *printed the letter George Washington wrote to the governor of Maryland announcing that the British had surrendered.* **What month and year was the paper printed?**

The American Revolutionary War ended when the British troops surrendered at Yorktown, Virginia. **What clues in this picture tell you that the troops are surrendering?**

Results of the Revolution

A lot had changed after the war. The 13 colonies became independent states, each with its own government. British laws could no longer stop people from moving west of the Appalachian Mountains. Many of the soldiers had traveled far away from their homes. Black and white men had fought together. Many slaves won their freedom by fighting in the Revolution. Many people freed their slaves because of the ideas of liberty that came out of the Revolution. States north of Maryland passed laws to end slavery. Maryland did not end slavery, but many African Americans did become free.

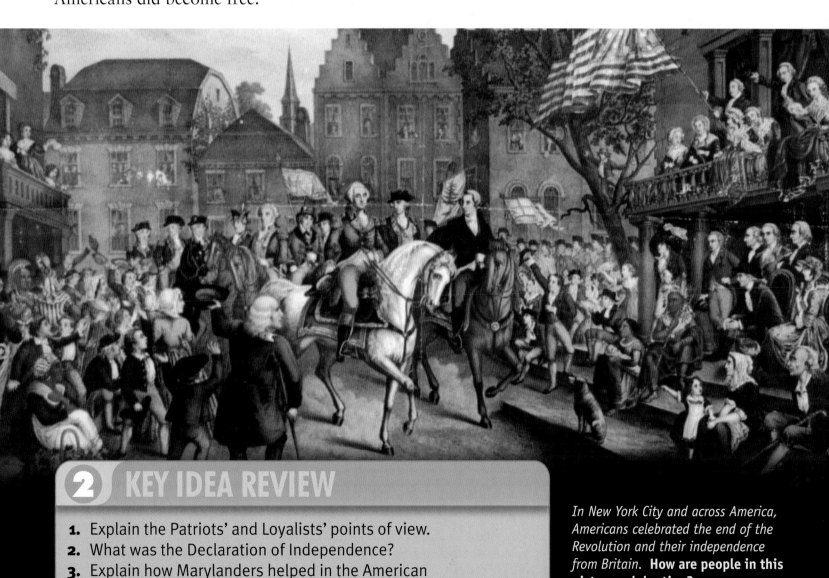

2 KEY IDEA REVIEW

1. Explain the Patriots' and Loyalists' points of view.
2. What was the Declaration of Independence?
3. Explain how Marylanders helped in the American Revolutionary War.
4. List three results of the Revolution.

In New York City and across America, Americans celebrated the end of the Revolution and their independence from Britain. **How are people in this picture celebrating?**

KEY IDEA

After winning independence, the United States of America formed its own government.

WORDS TO UNDERSTAND

amendment
capital
constitution
guarantee
individual
monarchy

Congress was meeting in Annapolis when George Washington announced he was leaving the military. He was elected president several years later.
What do you think the mood was like at this meeting?

A New Nation

As soon as the colonies declared independence in 1776, each new state wrote a constitution and set up its government. A *constitution* is a plan for government and the laws it will have. Representatives from all the states also met to set up a national government.

Maryland's State Government

Leaders in Maryland wrote a constitution for our state. It explained what powers the government would have and how the laws would be made. The governor would be the highest state leader. The General Assembly would have two parts—the State Senate and the House of Delegates. These two groups would make laws for the state.

The state constitution also said who could vote in Maryland. Only Christian men who owned property could vote. Non-Christians, poor men, women, slaves, and Indians could not vote. Free black men who owned property could vote.

A National Government

The states worked together to form a government for the new nation. Most Americans did not want a *monarchy* like England had. They did not want a king or queen to have all the power. At first, they wanted the states to have more power than the national government. They had just gotten rid of one very strong government, and they did not want another one.

Soon, Americans realized that they needed a stronger national government, with some real power over the states. They wanted the country to be strong and united to deal with all the problems they would face as a young nation.

Leaders from the states knew that to have a successful government, the country needed a new set of laws. They got together and wrote the Constitution of the United States. You will learn more about our government in a later chapter.

Thomas Johnson Jr. was the first governor of the state of Maryland.

The Maryland State House in Annapolis is where the General Assembly met in the past as well as today. **Why do you think the state house was built on a hill?**

137

The Constitution of the United States

Leaders from the states decided that the country needed a set of new laws. These men were later called our country's Founding Fathers. Can you guess why? They got together in Philadelphia, Pennsylvania, and wrote the Constitution of the United States. This new Constitution became the law for the whole country. These are the laws that still guide our country today, more than 200 years later. You will learn more about our government in a later chapter.

The Bill of Rights

After the U.S. Constitution was written, many Americans were worried that it did not protect their *individual* rights well enough. They wanted the rights of each person to be protected. They wanted an extra *guarantee*, or promise, that the new government could not take away people's rights. The writers added 10 *amendments* to the Constitution. These additions to the Constitution are called the Bill of Rights. You will read more about these rights in a later chapter.

Linking the Present to the Past

The amendments that make up the Bill of Rights are the first 10 amendments to the U.S. Constitution. Other amendments were added later. Even today, we sometimes add amendments to the Constitution. The men who wrote the Constitution knew Americans might want to make changes to it later on. They spelled out the way for this to happen.

The Battle of Bladensburg and the Burning of Washington

The British sailed up the Patuxent River and landed near Upper Marlboro in Prince George's County. They sent soldiers marching towards Washington, D.C.

Joshua Barney, a Marylander, and his navy men fought bravely at the Battle of Bladensburg. However, the British pushed on to the capital. They set fire to the White House, the Capitol, and the Naval Yard. This became known as the Burning of Washington. Many government officials *fled*, or ran away from, the city. Then the British headed toward Baltimore.

The Battle of Baltimore

The Battle of Baltimore was a turning point in the war. A *turning point* occurs when an important change happens. The Americans won, but it was not easy. General Samuel Smith was in charge of defending the city. He commanded the local militia. Many free blacks, slaves, young boys, and men joined with the militia to help defend the city against the British attack. Smith moved 60 large cannons to Fort McHenry at the mouth of Baltimore Harbor. He placed *lookouts*, or men who kept watch, and warships from North Point to Baltimore.

Joshua Barney

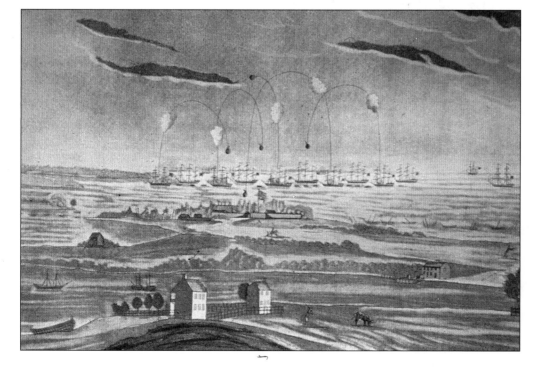

The Americans defended Fort McHenry during the Battle of Baltimore.
From where does this picture show the British firing cannon balls?

General Samuel Smith

Smith ordered all men who were not in the army, including free blacks and slaves, to come to Hampstead Hill (now Patterson Park in East Baltimore) to build forts. Baltimore's women made food for the workers. They helped nurse the wounded. They were not paid, but they wanted to help their city. Everyone joined in the effort to protect Baltimore.

Smith had 15,000 men ready to meet the enemies when they landed at North Point. The British started to march towards the city. At the same time, the British Navy moved ships around Fort McHenry. They began to attack the fort.

The Maryland soldiers forced the British to retreat at the Battle of Hampstead Hill. The Americans held Fort McHenry through a day and night of British bombing. The Americans had won, and the British left Baltimore.

The End of the War

After American troops won a second major battle in New York, the British wanted peace. The War of 1812 was over, and Marylanders could return to their normal lives.

British ships attacked Fort McHenry towards the end of the War of 1812. **How does this picture show that the fort was being attacked?**

Celebrating America

Sewing a Large American Flag

The commander at Fort McHenry wanted a U.S. flag to mark his fort. He wanted it to be huge, so the British could see it from far away. A group of army officers chose Mary Pickersgill to make the flag.

Pickersgill agreed to make a U.S. flag for the fort. She had made flags for ships before. Pickersgill, her mother, and her 13-year-old daughter measured, cut, and sewed 15 stars and stripes. However, there was not enough room in their home to sew the pieces together. They used the floor of a nearby building to sew the flag each evening by candlelight.

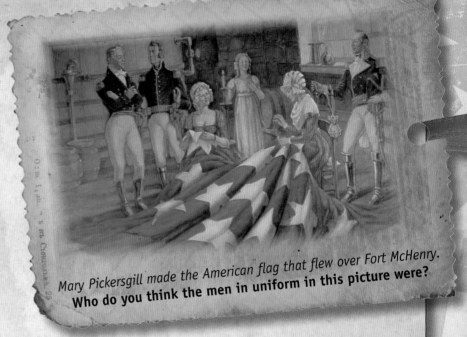

Mary Pickersgill made the American flag that flew over Fort McHenry. Who do you think the men in uniform in this picture were?

"The Star Spangled Banner"

An American lawyer named Francis Scott Key was onboard a British ship in Baltimore Harbor at the same time the British were bombing Fort McHenry. He was trying to win the release of an American taken prisoner by the British. As night came, the bombs continued to fall. When daylight returned, Key saw that the large American flag that Pickersgill had sewn was still flying over the fort. He knew the Americans had defended the fort successfully. To celebrate, Key wrote a poem about it on the back of a letter he had in his pocket. He sent his poem to a printer. In just a few days, the words were put to the music of an old English song. It was called "The Star Spangled Banner." Many years later, it became our national anthem. An **anthem** is a song of praise or joy.

Francis Scott Key

1 KEY IDEA REVIEW

1. Why did the War of 1812 begin?
2. Name two important battles that took place during the War of 1812.
3. How did the War of 1812 end?

KEY IDEA

Industries like farming, fishing, and manufacturing helped Maryland grow.

WORDS TO UNDERSTAND

diverse
fertile
gristmill
import
manufacturing
textile mill

Growth Across the Land

Maryland grew a lot after the War of 1812. Families were having children, and many people, especially Europeans, were moving to Maryland.

Southern Maryland

Most people in Southern Maryland were farmers who grew tobacco. Many did all their own work. Rich people who owned plantations had slaves. Most African Americans in Southern Maryland were enslaved. They helped create the region's wealth. Upper Marlboro was an important town in Southern Maryland.

Eastern Shore

Most people on the Eastern Shore were also farmers. They grew wheat and other crops. Some farmers freed their slaves because they believed slavery was wrong. Others freed slaves because it cost less to hire workers only when they needed them. Some farmers still depended on slaves to harvest their crops.

Many free African Americans became farmers or farm workers. Others owned and worked on fishing boats. Some were skilled craftsmen.

People on the Eastern Shore also did other jobs. Craftsmen made everything from shoes to furniture. They made pots and pans and shoes for horses. A lot of men worked in shipyards, building and repairing ships.

Baltimore was developing into a business and industrial center at this time. **What do you see in this picture that shows this?**

Other people worked on the water, harvesting seafood, especially oysters that lived in the Chesapeake Bay and in rivers near the bay.

Easton became the most important town on the Eastern Shore. The state government opened offices there to serve the people living east of the Chesapeake Bay.

Western Maryland

Western Maryland was no longer a frontier. People from other parts of Maryland and other countries were settling there. Germans and Scotch-Irish settled in the region.
The Scotch-Irish had moved from Scotland to Ireland and then to America. Hagerstown and Frederick were important towns in Western Maryland. Farms spread across the *fertile* valleys, where the soil was good for growing crops.

Central Maryland

Many people found jobs in mining and manufacturing in Central Maryland. *Manufacturing* is the production of goods. *Gristmills* made grain into flour. *Textile mills* made cloth for clothing and sails for ships. Local mines produced iron. Iron was made into nails and other products.

Joseph Ellicott and his brothers built mills by the falls along the Patapsco River. Some mill towns had housing for the workers. These towns had stores, where people could buy what they needed, and churches, where they could worship.

Central Maryland had two main cities—Annapolis and Baltimore. Annapolis had fine shops, many lawyers and professional people, and government workers. A lot of people, including free blacks and slaves, worked at skilled crafts, in businesses, and at the port. Annapolis had good music and theater for the people to enjoy.

Farming was very important in Southern Maryland, the Eastern Shore, and Western Maryland. **What work are these farmers doing?**

Baltimore

Baltimore was the state's business center. There were lots of jobs there. Many free black people came to Baltimore. Slaves escaped to Baltimore because they could disappear in the crowds. People from European countries and other states also came to Baltimore. It was the most diverse place in Maryland. **Diverse** means having many different characteristics.

Some merchants and bankers became very wealthy. They put their money into other new businesses. The work of these men helped Baltimore grow. Merchants shipped grain through the port of Baltimore to other states and to the West Indies. New banks opened.

Shipbuilders, captains, and sailors lived near the water. Workers hauled goods to and from the port. They loaded and unloaded the ships. They built roads, houses, warehouses, and wagons. Skilled craftspeople made many of the things people needed to live. It was no longer necessary to import as many goods from Great Britain. To **import** means to bring goods in from another country.

Some women worked to earn money. They ran boarding houses, where people new to the city could live. Some did laundry. Some did sewing.

Baltimore was a busy city with a lot of jobs for people to do. **What do you see in this picture of Baltimore?**

Chapter 6: Life in the New State

The National Road

Families began to move into the Ohio River Valley. They raised cattle and grew grain. They wanted to sell their dairy products, meat, and crops in eastern cities, but it was hard to move things across the Appalachian Mountains to the East Coast.

To make things easier, the government built a road that went across several states. It was wide enough for wagons and stagecoaches. It was called the National Road.

The National Road started in Cumberland, Maryland. It connected towns in several states. Over time, the road stretched farther west. Soon it reached Illinois.

Many people worked on building the road. They worked all day, chopping down trees and digging paths through thick grass and over high ridges. They worked until their muscles ached. It was hard work to cut through the mountain rocks.

When the National Road opened, stagecoaches and wagons carried people and goods from the city and countryside. Farmers drove herds of cattle, sheep, and pigs along the road to market. People sent letters and newspapers from towns in the East to people in the West.

The National Road was a little higher in the middle than along the sides. This allowed water and snow to drain off into the ditches on each side.

The National Road stretched from Maryland to Illinois. **Can you name three cities the National Road passed through?**

Canals

Canals also connected places. It was easier to move heavy goods by water than across the land. People built canals to connect one river to another. Then they had an all-water route to move supplies. Maryland built two successful canals.

The two canals were the Chesapeake and Ohio Canal and the Chesapeake and Delaware Canal. The Chesapeake and Ohio Canal connected Washington, D.C., to Western Maryland. It was nicknamed the C&O Canal. The Chesapeake and Delaware Canal linked the Delaware Bay and the Chesapeake Bay. Ships still use this canal today.

Canal boats had flat bottoms and were very long. They did not have engines. Mules pulled them along with heavy ropes. The mules walked along a towpath beside the canal. Many young boys wanted the job of driving the mules along the path.

Often an entire family lived on a canal boat. They made their living hauling goods back and forth along the canal. The canal boat had a small cabin in the back with bunk beds. The mules slept in a stable in the front of the boat.

Projects like the C&O Canal were often paid for with the sale of lottery tickets. **How much did this lottery ticket cost?**

Mules pulled canal boats. **How did the mules pull the boats along?**

Linking the Present to the Past

Shipping goods across the country is still very important today. Large trucks and trains carry goods to small towns and big cities. Ships carry goods to cities located on rivers, bays, and oceans.

156

Railroads

At about the same time workers began building the Chesapeake and Ohio Canal, other workers began building the Baltimore and Ohio Railroad. Railroads were very new at the time. The B&O was the first railroad in the United States.

Men worked quickly to build the B&O. By 1830, the tracks ran from Baltimore to Ellicott's Mills. Next, the tracks reached Frederick and then Cumberland. Later still, the tracks reached Wheeling, Virginia, on the Ohio River.

Steam trains could carry heavy coal from Cumberland to the rest of Maryland. This meant places that did not have their own supply of coal could now get it more easily. Many towns grew because the supply of coal allowed them to open new industries. For instance, the town of Laurel built mills and a machine shop. The new industries made jobs for hundreds of people.

What Do You Think ?

Roads, canals, and railroads were important for moving goods 150 years ago. We still use all of these methods of transportation today. How do you think we will move goods 150 years from now?

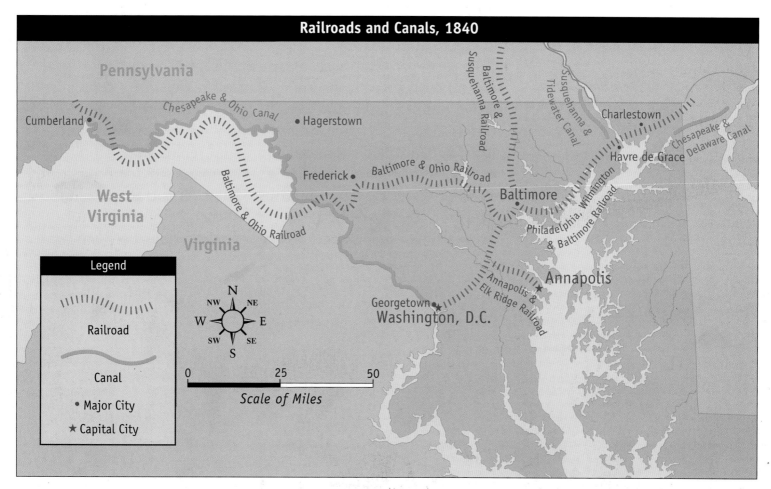

Railroads and Canals, 1840

Many new railroads and canals were built. **Can you name one railroad and one canal?**

Factories and Cities Grow

Cities grow.

More people move to cities.

Factories make and sell more goods.

Factories need more workers.

Cities and Towns

With all the advances in transportation—roads, railroads, and canals—Maryland's cities grew. New transportation routes made it possible for companies to ship their goods to places far away. Factories made and sold more goods. More and larger factories were built in our cities.

New factories needed new workers, so more people began to move to cities. This meant that more food had to be imported from the farms. All the new transportation routes and ways of moving goods made it easier to bring food to the cities. All the new people also needed new houses.

Baltimore Grows

Baltimore was the largest and most industrialized city in Maryland. It grew from 13,500 people in 1790 to almost 170,000 in 1850. That's like having your class grow from 30 students to almost 380!

The success of railroads meant that a lot of engines, railroad cars, and tracks had to be built. Baltimore became a center for railroad building. A lot of people came to Baltimore to build rails and railroad cars. Other industries grew in Baltimore as well. Shipyards continued to manufacture and repair ships. Textile factories, which made cloth, grew. Companies made flour from the grain imported from the farms. Then ships transported the flour as far away as South America. Other Baltimore factories processed sugar and coffee that came from places far away.

Baltimore was a growing city in the mid-1800s. **What museum is shown in this picture?**

Other Cities Grow

Baltimore was not the only city that grew during these years. Another was Frederick, which became a busy manufacturing center. Goods made from iron and glass were manufactured there. There were also wagon shops, potteries, and breweries. A brewery is a factory that makes beer. Local farmers could buy tools to work the land. Many pioneer families traveling west stocked up on or bought all of their supplies in Frederick. People bought goods made of heavy iron or breakable glass as far west as possible so they would not have as far to transport them.

Hagerstown and Cumberland built industries that made good use of the coal that was mined in the western part of the state. Local people as well as families traveling west could buy goods in these towns.

All the big industries in Maryland cities needed workers. Many African Americans worked in industries here. People from other countries also came to Maryland looking for work. During the years between the end of the War of 1812 and 1850, a lot of workers came from Germany and Ireland. They came to Maryland and many other parts of our country.

Edgar Allan Poe
1809–1849

Edgar Allan Poe wrote short stories and poems that people still read today. He lived in Baltimore and several other cities, including New York and Richmond. The house in Baltimore where Poe lived is a museum today.

Poe wrote stories for ordinary people to enjoy. He wrote horror stories and mystery stories. His first famous mystery story was called "The Murders in Rue Morgue." Poe influenced writers around the world.

Poe also wrote many poems that became famous. One of his most famous is called "The Raven." A raven is a large black bird.

Edgar Allan Poe died in Baltimore. He is buried in the Westminster Burying Ground. Since 1949, on the night of Poe's birthday, a mysterious stranger comes into the cemetery and leaves a bottle of brandy and three red roses on Poe's grave.

Today, Baltimore's football team is named the Ravens.

Immigrants did most of the work to build the canals. **From what is shown in this picture, can you list two jobs the workers did?**

Immigrant Workers

American industries were growing quickly, but there were not enough workers to fill all the new jobs. Companies started spreading the word to European countries that people could find jobs in America. Many Europeans left their homes and families to come to the United States. They called it the "Land of Opportunity."

Immigrants from Europe came on ships to Baltimore and Annapolis. *Immigrants* are people who move from one country to another country to live. These workers, farmers, and craftsmen helped build our state and our nation. Often they had very difficult lives.

Irish Immigrants

In Ireland, many families were poor. Some Irish people survived on potatoes, a crop that grew well there.

A disease that made the potato plants rot lasted for several years. People in Ireland began to starve. Many left Ireland to come to the United States. Some came to Maryland.

Many of the Irish immigrants had been too poor to go to school in Ireland. When they arrived in America, they had to take jobs that did not require an education. Irish men helped build the roads, canals, and railroads that were so important to our young nation. Irish women cleaned and did laundry for other families. Some Irish children also worked long hours. They gave the pennies they earned to their families to buy food or pay rent.

Colleges

Two early Maryland colleges are still educating students today. Washington College, the first in Maryland, opened in Chestertown. Two years later, St. John's College opened in Annapolis.

The Medical College of Maryland opened in Baltimore to train doctors. A dental school followed. These later became part of the University of Maryland.

St. John's College still educates students today.

Early Schools in Maryland

Elizabeth Seton

Elizabeth Seton started St. Joseph's School for Girls in Baltimore. She wanted to teach girls. She was very committed to the Catholic religion. After working in her school, she decided to become a nun. Long after she died, the Roman Catholic Church made her a saint. She was the first person in the United States to be made a Catholic saint.

William Watkins started Watkins' Academy for black students. His niece, Frances Watkins Harper, studied there. Later, she became a teacher. She wrote poetry that many people still like to read today.

Frances Watkins Harper

3 KEY IDEA REVIEW

1. What transportation improvements were made during this time?
2. How did transportation help Maryland cities grow?
3. Why was America called the "Land of Opportunity"?
4. How did education change during this time?

Go to the Source

Read "The Star Spangled Banner"

As you read, Francis Scott Key wrote a poem about the War of 1812 that became our national anthem. This is a copy of the first draft of "The Star Spangled Banner." The first verse is copied below.

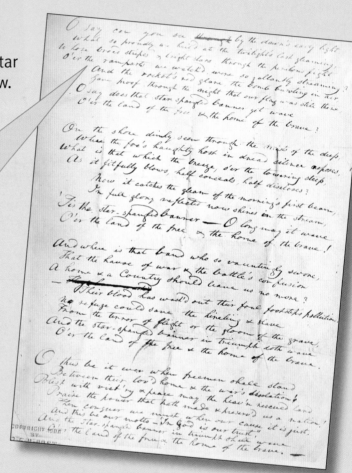

> O say, can you see, by the dawn's early light,
> What so proudly we hailed at the twilight's last gleaming,
> Whose broad stripes and bright stars, through the perilous fight,
> O'er the ramparts we watched, were so gallantly streaming?
> And the rockets' red glare, the bombs bursting in air,
> Gave proof through the night that our flag was still there.
> O say, does that star spangled banner yet wave,
> O'er the land of the free, and the home of the brave?

LOOK	THINK	DECIDE
What can you describe about the appearance of Key's draft?	In the first verse, why is it good that the "flag was still there"?	Key wrote "The Star Spangled Banner" as he watched Americans successfully defend Fort McHenry. Why do you think it is possible for people like Key to write works of praise when they are experiencing hard times?

Spotlighting Geography

War of 1812 Battles in Maryland

Look at the map below. Where in Maryland did major battles take place during the War of 1812? Which battle happened first? Which happened second and third?

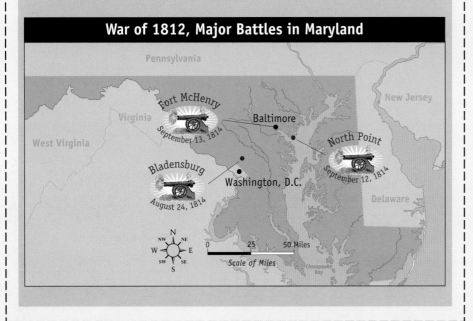

War of 1812, Major Battles in Maryland

Pennsylvania

Fort McHenry
September 13, 1814

Baltimore

Virginia

West Virginia

North Point
September 12, 1814

Bladensburg
August 24, 1814

Washington, D.C.

Delaware

New Jersey

Chesapeake Bay

0 25 50 Miles

Scale of Miles

Reviewing What You Read

1. What war did the Americans and British fight over land and trading rights?
2. List three changes that happened within society during this period.
3. Describe one job in Maryland at this time.
4. In your own words, restate the Big Idea of this chapter.
5. Compare transportation during this period to transportation today.
6. Write a concluding sentence summarizing this chapter.

Becoming a Better Reader

Find the Main Idea

When reading nonfiction information, good readers always keep the main idea of what they are reading in mind. Thinking about the main idea helps readers better understand the new information they gather as they read. The main idea can be found by reading chapter and lesson titles and headings and subheadings. What is the main idea of this chapter? Write a paragraph stating the main idea and three supporting ideas.

The Civil War

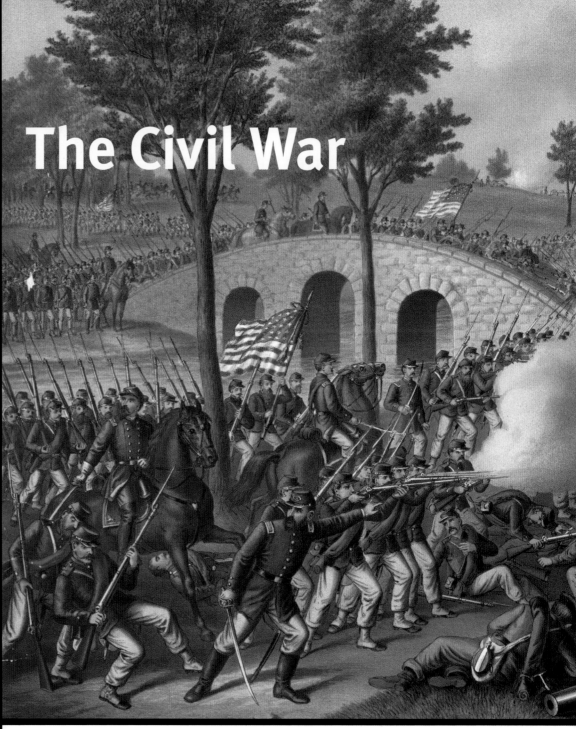

What's the Big Idea?

The country and our state were divided by the Civil War.

Many battles, including the Battle of Antietam, took place in Maryland during the Civil War. **How did war differ in the past from war today?**

Timeline of Events

1820

1830

1840

1830–1865
Some slaves escape to freedom on the Underground Railroad.

1830–1860
Anti-slavery groups grow in the North.

1833
Maryland in Liberia is founded.

168

Chapter 7

Slavery and other problems were tearing our country in two. The North and the South had many differences. The North depended on industry, while the South depended on agriculture. Many powerful people in the South used slaves to work on their plantations.

After Abraham Lincoln was elected president, many Southern states left the United States and started their own country, so they could make their own laws. This caused a terrible war. President Lincoln did all that he could to bring our country back together.

1859
John Brown leads a rebellion at Harpers Ferry.

1865
Lincoln is shot. He dies the next day.

1860–1861
Southern states leave the Union.

1870
The 15th Amendment gives African American men the right to vote.

1861–1865
Civil War

1850

1860

1870

1852
Uncle Tom's Cabin is published.

1861
• Abraham Lincoln becomes president.
• The Baltimore Riot

1862
Battle of Antietam

1864
• Lincoln is re-elected as president
• Slavery becomes illegal in Maryland.

1863
• The Emancipation Proclamation ends slavery in the South.
• Battle of Gettysburg

KEY IDEA

Many differences, especially different ideas about slavery, caused problems between the northern and southern states.

WORDS TO UNDERSTAND

auction
equality
laborer
minister
overseer
rebel

A Nation Divided

By the middle of the 1800s, parts of our state and country had grown and changed in different ways. These differences would eventually lead to a horrible war.

Industry and Agriculture

In the North, industries and business became very powerful. The cities were growing. The most powerful men lived in the cities.

After Americans fought for freedom during the American Revolution, the northern states made slavery against the law. Many northerners were farmers on small farms. They did not need or want slaves on their farms.

In the South, most of the wealth still came from farming. Cotton was the main crop. Slaves did a lot of the hard work. Many of the powerful people owned plantations. Cities in the South were smaller than cities in the North.

Because of all their differences, the North and the South wanted different things from the government. The North wanted the government to help business and industry. The South wanted it to help agriculture.

People in the North and the South had different ways of making money. **What did the North and what did the South mostly depend on to make money?**

The North

The South

States Make Decisions About Slavery

The biggest issue that divided the North and the South was slavery. Most Northerners said that slavery was wrong. They said Southerners should not own slaves.

The national government let each state decide whether to allow slavery or not. States that did not allow slavery were called "free states." States that allowed slavery were called "slave states." Maryland was a slave state. However, many free blacks lived here.

Many Southerners believed they needed slaves to grow the cotton that brought wealth to the South. For 200 years, enslaved workers produced crops that could be sold. Most white Southerners did not want to end slavery.

Different Ideas in Maryland

Maryland is located between the northern states and southern states. Maryland was part North and part South. All parts of Maryland had some people who favored the North and others who favored the South. Many people in Maryland did business with both the North and the South. More than anything, most Marylanders wanted to avoid war. War would hurt their business. Also, they knew a lot of battles would be fought in our state because it was in between the North and the South.

Wealthy Southerners owned plantations, such as this one, where they grew cotton. It took many workers to plant, care for, and pick the cotton. **What clues does this picture give you about why rich Southerners did not want slavery to end?**

171

Slavery was disappearing in Baltimore. This free African American man sold oysters in Baltimore. **Where do you think he is walking from and where do you think he is going?**

Northern, Western, and central Maryland were like the North in many ways. Most of the farms were small, and most farmers did not own slaves. Most of the German immigrants who lived there were against slavery. They had small farms and did all their own work. Baltimore had grown into a big city. It depended on industry and trade for its wealth. Baltimore was like a city in the North. Slavery was disappearing there. Most blacks in Baltimore were free.

Southern Maryland and the Eastern Shore were more like the South. These two regions depended on agriculture. While the most important crop farther south was cotton, the most important crop in Maryland was tobacco. The people who owned large tobacco farms depended on slave labor to plant and harvest their crops. The Eastern Shore had smaller farms that produced a greater variety of products, such as wheat, corn, and vegetables. Some of those farmers had slaves. Many did not.

Life As a Slave

The Declaration of Independence said "all men are created equal." But enslaved people were not considered equal to other people. They were thought of as property. Slavery was a terrible part of the history of Maryland and our whole nation.

Slaves at Work

Most enslaved people worked on large plantations or smaller farms. Men, women, and children over the age of six planted seeds, took care of the plants, and harvested crops. They worked 12 or 14 hours a day in the hot sun or the rain.

Some enslaved people learned skilled crafts. They worked as carpenters, blacksmiths, and boot makers. In Maryland, some slaves worked in iron mines and other industries. A few worked in shops and businesses. Some cooked and cleaned and took care of children in the master's house. The work of enslaved people added to the state's wealth.

Tobacco was the main crop in Southern Maryland. **What work are these slaves doing?**

Members of African American slave families often lived near one another. However, there was always a risk they could be sold to people who lived farther away from their relatives. **How many children are in this picture?**

Slave Families

Like all children, enslaved children had a mother and a father. Many had sisters and brothers, aunts and uncles, grandmothers and grandfathers. Often family members lived near each other. But, at any time, an owner might sell a slave to someone who lived far away.

At slave *auctions*, slaves were sold to the highest bidders, who would pay the most for them. Mothers were dragged from their children. Brothers and sisters were torn apart. Sometimes they never saw each other again.

Enslaved people did not have as many opportunities or choices as whites and free blacks. They could not go to school. They could not choose their jobs. They could not protect their families.

"My brothers and sisters were bid off first . . . while my mother . . . held me by the hand. Then I was offered. My mother pushed through the crowd to the spot where [her master] was standing. She fell at his knees, [begging] him . . . to buy her baby as well as herself."

—Josiah Henson,
a Maryland slave

African Americans were sometimes separated from their families when they were sold at slave auctions. **Can you describe what is happening in this picture?**

Chapter 7: The Civil War

Punishment

Most Marylanders did not think slave masters should treat slaves badly. But most of the time, no one stopped the slave owners from beating or whipping slaves.

Sometimes an owner who had a lot of slaves hired an *overseer* to make sure the slaves did their work. If an enslaved person did something the overseer did not like, the overseer might also punish the slave.

Slaves Rebelled

It is no surprise that enslaved people did not like living as slaves. Many of them *rebelled*. Some rose up against their owners. Many more just ran away.

Some slaves did not want to risk the punishment they would get if they were caught planning a rebellion or trying to escape. Often they just decided not to work very hard. That was another way to rebel against slavery.

What Do You Think?

Why is it important to remember the terrible, sad parts of history as well as the good parts?

Sometimes slaves received horrible beatings and other punishments.
How is this slave being punished?

Many former slaves had gained their freedom and were working hard to build a new life. **What is this former slave couple doing outside their cabin?**

Free Blacks

Across Maryland and America, many African Americans were free. Some blacks had been free from the earliest colonial years. After the American Revolution, many more became free. Some earned freedom because they fought in the army. Some became free when slave owners decided that slavery was wrong and freed their slaves. Quaker families freed all of their slaves.

Throughout the North, states passed laws ending slavery. In Maryland, some enslaved people worked, saved money, and then bought their freedom. Many slaves ran away. Some went North. Some hid in big cities like Baltimore, where no one knew them.

Free blacks built churches and schools in cities like Annapolis and Baltimore and in some small towns. Some opened businesses. A few were teachers and religious leaders. Many were **laborers**, or workers, who worked hard to get enough money to buy food and pay rent.

Outside of cities, most free blacks were farmers. Some were able to buy land. Others worked for pay on someone else's land. Some were craftspeople, who sold the things they made.

As the years passed, more and more African Americans in Maryland became free. Just before the Civil War began, about half were free. Baltimore had the largest free African American community in the whole country.

Tough Times for Free Blacks

Free blacks had only some of the rights that whites enjoyed. They were not enslaved, but they did not have full *equality* either. Even in states farther north, free blacks did not have equal rights.

In Maryland, free African Americans could own property. They could be legally married. They could travel around the state. However, sometimes they had to show papers to prove they were free. Free blacks could not vote or hold public office. African Americans were not allowed to do some jobs.

Maryland in Liberia

To try to build a better life for themselves, a small number of free African Americans decided to leave the United States and establish a new home in West Africa, where many of their ancestors had come from. They founded a nation called Liberia. People from Maryland settled nearby. They called their smaller settlement Maryland in Liberia. Nineteen men, women, and children sailed from Baltimore to Africa. Within four years, there were 400 people living in the Maryland in Liberia settlement. The Methodist minister Daniel Coker was a leader of the settlement. A *minister* leads church services.

Free blacks could own land in Maryland. **What do you think this family is selling?**

1 KEY IDEA REVIEW

1. Why was the United States, as well as Maryland, divided?
2. Describe what life was like for slaves.
3. Describe what life was like for free blacks.

LESSON ② Working to End Slavery

KEY IDEA

Many people worked hard to bring an end to slavery and make everyone free.

WORDS TO UNDERSTAND

abolitionist
anti-slavery
overland
rebellion
route
treason

Many Thought Slavery Was Wrong

As you read in the last lesson, Americans believed slavery was wrong. They believed slavery did not fit with the principles they had fought for during the American Revolution. Some religious people believed all human beings were equal in the eyes of God. Therefore, many people believed no human being should own another human being.

As you know, the northern states passed laws to end slavery soon after the American Revolution. In Maryland, laws to end slavery did not pass. However, over the years, there was less and less slavery here.

People across the country who worked to end slavery were called *abolitionists*. They were male and female, black and white, young and old. They shared a belief that slavery was wrong.

The message of the abolitionists was not always well received around the country. **What happened to this group of abolitionists who had come to speak at a church?**

Rebellion at Harpers Ferry

John Brown, a white abolitionist, led a rebellion. A *rebellion* is an armed fight against people in power. He and a group of men stole guns from an army storehouse near Harpers Ferry, Virginia, a town just across the border from Maryland. Brown planned to give the guns to slaves, who could then fight for their freedom. The Maryland militia helped capture John Brown and the others. Brown was hanged for the crime of *treason*, or plotting against the government.

John Brown and other men stole weapons to give to slaves from a storehouse in Harpers Ferry, Virginia. **How did the Maryland militia respond to this rebellion?**

What Do You Think ?

John Brown believed that slavery was evil. He decided to fight against it by killing people who supported it.

Throughout history, men and women have used violence to try to bring about change. Do you think it is right or wrong to use violence to try to cause change?

Underground Railroad A Way to Freedom

Most people trying to escape to the North traveled at night. They followed the North Star in the night sky. That small star always showed them which way was north.

People had run away as long as there had been slavery. After the 1830s, abolitionist societies grew in the North. One way abolitionists helped enslaved people get their freedom was by working on the Underground Railroad, which was not a railroad at all. The Underground Railroad was the system of secret routes slaves used to escape as well as the abolitionists who helped the slaves along their journey north. Many members of abolitionist societies provided housing and transportation for escaping slaves.

Abolitionists who helped the runaways were called "conductors." They hid slaves in their homes, barns, and churches. These safe hiding places were called "stations." Other conductors provided transportation from one place to another.

People also used some public places during their escapes. There were Underground Railroad stations all the way to Canada.

Slaves traveled north in different ways. A lot of people walked, others rode on real trains, and some rode in wagons. Many sailed up the Chesapeake Bay. The bay was a route to freedom. A *route* is a course of travel. Some ship captains were conductors on the Underground Railroad. After the ships reached the northern end of the Chesapeake Bay, the slaves walked *overland*, or across the land, through Delaware into Pennsylvania, which was a free state.

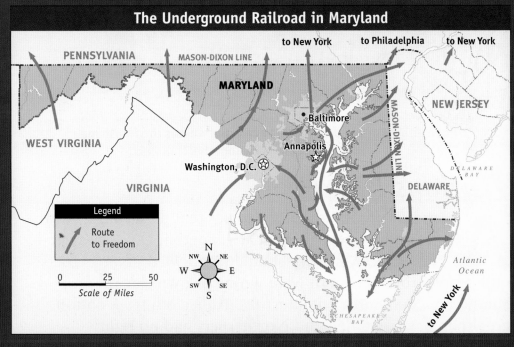

The Underground Railroad in Maryland

This map shows the different routes Maryland slaves used to escape to freedom on the Underground Railroad. Some of the arrows point south because some slaves sailed out of the Chesapeake Bay to the Atlantic Ocean and then sailed north.
Which direction did all of the routes eventually lead?

2 KEY IDEA REVIEW

1. Why did abolitionists believe slavery was wrong?
2. What was the Underground Railroad?
3. Name three abolitionists.

Ann Maria Weems Escapes

Ann Maria Weems was born to enslaved parents in Rockville, Maryland. Four of her brothers were sold away from the family to slave owners farther south. After that, an abolitionist from Washington, D.C., helped Weems escape when she was about 15 years old. First, he had her kidnapped from the owner's house. Then, he hid her in his attic for four weeks, while local police and slave catchers hunted for her. A newspaper advertisement offered $500 for her return.

A "conductor" from Philadelphia came to Washington, D.C., to pick up Weems. Weems was dressed as a coach boy. She helped the conductor with his coach and horses. She was called "Joe Wright." Weems and the conductor traveled by coach through Maryland and into Pennsylvania. If they had been caught, Weems would have been returned to slavery, and her conductor would have been arrested.

KEY IDEA

The hostility between the North and South resulted in a civil war.

WORDS TO UNDERSTAND

assassinate
civil war
occupy
riot
secede
volunteer

This cartoon made fun of all of the men who ran for president in 1860.
What are three of the men tearing apart and what is the fourth man trying to glue back together?

Tensions Build

Americans argued about the issues that divided the North and South. Lawmakers in Washington, D.C., disagreed about whether slavery should be allowed. Northerners said people from the South were wrong to own slaves. Southerners said northern industries made cloth from cotton grown by slaves, so they said Northerners had no right to complain.

People were angry. The more abolitionists attacked slavery, the more determined slave owners were to defend slavery. They said they didn't want Northerners telling them what to do about slavery or anything else.

Abraham Lincoln Becomes President

The United States held an election for a new president. Slavery was the big issue that everyone talked about. Four men ran for president. Abraham Lincoln, a lawyer from Illinois, was elected. Most people in the North voted for him.

Lincoln was against slavery. Most people in the South believed Lincoln would do away with slavery. They were really angry that Lincoln was the new president.

Abraham Lincoln was elected president of the United States.

The South Secedes

Across the South, people decided they did not want to be a part of this country any longer. One by one, the Southern states *seceded* from the United States and formed their own country. They called themselves the Confederate States of America or the Confederacy. The Northern states, which still called themselves the United States, were also called the North or the Union. There were four slave states that did not leave the Union, which were called border states. Maryland was one of them.

After Abraham Lincoln was elected president, many Southern states seceded from the Union. **How does this cartoon show the secession of the Southern states?**

War Begins

The situation in America was very tense. President Lincoln said Americans were not allowed to break up their country. The Confederacy wanted to be on its own. Its men were ready to fight. Soon, a *civil war*, a war between people in the same country, began. Lincoln said his reason for going to war was to save the Union.

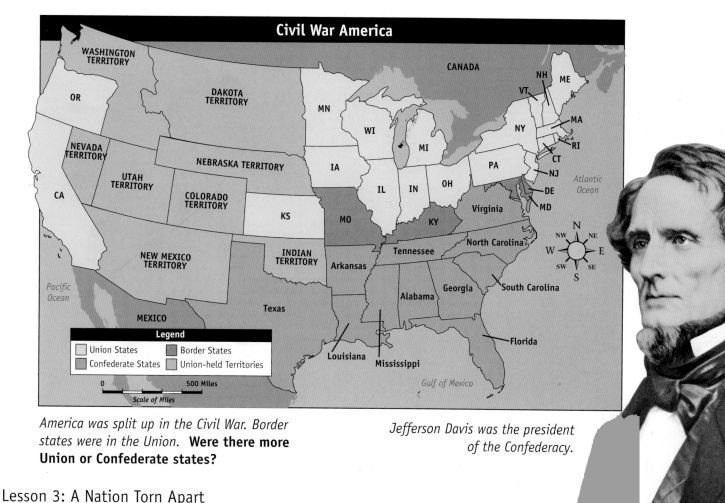

Civil War America

America was split up in the Civil War. Border states were in the Union. **Were there more Union or Confederate states?**

Jefferson Davis was the president of the Confederacy.

Lesson 3: A Nation Torn Apart

The Civil War in Maryland

There was a lot of fighting in Maryland because of where our state is located. Northern troops had to go through Maryland to get to the South. Southern troops came into Maryland to try to drive the Union soldiers back up north.

Many Marylanders fought in the Civil War. Most fought for the Union. Some fought for the Confederacy. Sometimes families were divided. Sometimes brothers fought against each other.

A State Divided

During the Civil War, most Marylanders favored the North, but some favored the South. A lot of the businessmen who did business with companies farther north did not want the country to split in two because it would hurt their business. Most small farmers, who did not have slaves, also favored the Union. All abolitionists, of course, favored the Union and hoped that Lincoln would end slavery.

Many Civil War battles took place in Maryland. **In what part of the state did most of the battles take place?**

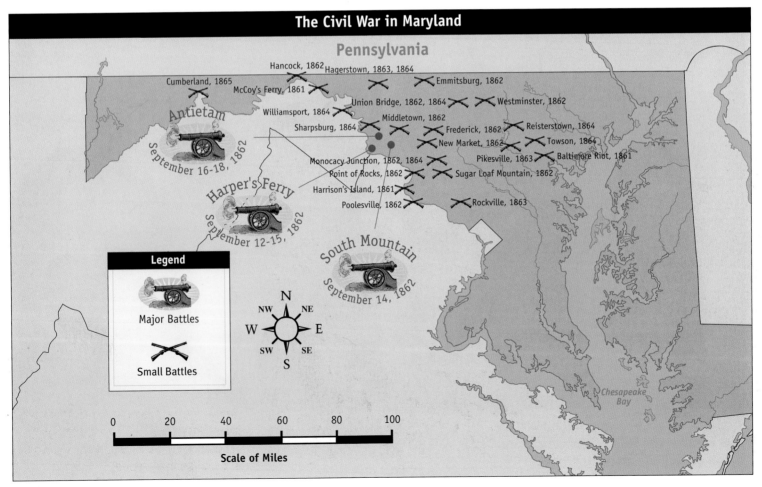

The Civil War in Maryland

Pennsylvania

Hancock, 1862   Hagerstown, 1863, 1864
Cumberland, 1865   Emmitsburg, 1862
McCoy's Ferry, 1861
Union Bridge, 1862, 1864   Westminster, 1862
Williamsport, 1864
Antietam   Sharpsburg, 1864   Middletown, 1862
September 16-18, 1862   Frederick, 1862   Reisterstown, 1864
New Market, 1862   Towson, 1864
Monocacy Junction, 1862, 1864   Pikesville, 1863   Baltimore Riot, 1861
Harper's Ferry   Point of Rocks, 1862   Sugar Loaf Mountain, 1862
September 12-15, 1862   Harrison's Island, 1861
Poolesville, 1862   Rockville, 1863

South Mountain
September 14, 1862

Legend

Major Battles

Small Battles

N NW NE W E SW SE S

Chesapeake Bay

0   20   40   60   80   100

Scale of Miles

A number of Marylanders favored the Confederacy. Some of them had slaves and worried that Lincoln would end slavery. Some did business in the South. Others believed the Union should not force the South to remain part of the country. Some families in all parts of the state had relatives in states farther south, like Virginia. Some of them also took the side of the Confederacy.

The Baltimore Riot

Union soldiers from Massachusetts traveled south to defend the nation's capital. They had to pass through Baltimore on their way.

Some Marylanders who supported the South did not want Union troops to come through their state. They attacked the troops. Before the street fighting ended, 16 people had been killed. These were the first deaths of the Civil War.

After the *riot*, the Union army stayed in Baltimore to make sure there was no more trouble. The Union also wanted to control the land next to Washington, D.C.

Tensions were high as a group of soldiers from Massachusetts passed through Baltimore on their way to Washington, D.C. **What happened?**

The Battle of Antietam

One of the most terrible battles of the Civil War took place in Maryland. Soldiers from the North and South fought in a field south of Hagerstown, near Antietam Creek. Before the day was over, 23,000 soldiers lay dead or wounded. It was the bloodiest one-day battle of the whole war.

Neither side won the Battle of Antietam. Confederate General Robert E. Lee's army retreated into Virginia. The Northerners did not follow them. Both sides mourned their dead.

The Battle of Gettysburg

The next year the Confederate army returned to western Maryland. This time they marched through Maryland into southern Pennsylvania. Union troops met them at a town called Gettysburg. The Union won a big victory at Gettysburg. It was the turning point of the Civil War.

The Battle of Gettysburg was a turning point in the Civil War. The Union won the battle. **Can you describe the scene shown in this painting?**

A Soldier's Life

Many young men had joined the army thinking the war would be exciting and short. They dreamed of being brave heroes. But the war was not how they imagined it would be. Soldiers spent most days sitting in camp, waiting for a battle. When a battle happened, it was often horrible. Men were shot and killed. Some lost arms or legs.

Often the armies were not able to give soldiers the things they needed to live. Sometimes soldiers ran out of food. Sometimes they did not have shoes or other supplies. Sometimes soldiers raided homes and farms to steal what they needed.

Diseases killed a lot of soldiers. Some army camps were not clean. Human waste lay all around. The water supply was often dirty. Men got sick and died.

Not all soldiers were men. Boys as young as 13 left home for adventure or to escape bad conditions. Sometimes the boys were killed in battle. Boys who were too young to fight sometimes played drums or bugles while the soldiers marched. Sometimes even those young boys were killed.

Sergeant Major Christian Fleetwood of Maryland was awarded the Congressional Medal of Honor for bravery in battle.

A bugle was used in the war to give military commands since it could be heard above all of the gunfire. **How is a bugle similar to and different from a trumpet?**

In this painting, a Union soldier is sleeping by the campfire after writing a letter home. **What is he dreaming about?**

At the time of the Civil War, photography was very new. In previous wars, people's descriptions were all that recorded what had happened. Early photography used a lot of heavy equipment. It took a very long time to develop pictures. However, people could now see with their own eyes what happened at an event by looking at a picture. Today, we can take pictures of events with small digital cameras and then e-mail the pictures around the world in a few minutes. Do you think photos make a difference in how people feel about what is happening in the world?

Women and the War Effort

Women helped in the Civil War in many ways. When men went to war, many women took over their work on farms and in shops. They helped keep the country going while the men were fighting.

Some women volunteered to nurse wounded soldiers. To *volunteer* means to work without being paid. They worked long hours in overcrowded hospitals. They made clothes and bandages for the soldiers. Some women served as spies. Harriet Tubman worked as a spy for the Union army. A few women even dressed up as men and joined the army.

Women suffered just as the men did. They lost sons, husbands, fathers, and brothers. It was a very sad time for everyone.

Women helped in the Civil War in different ways. The women in the bottom picture were nurses, who took care of wounded soldiers. **How did the woman on the left in the top picture help out in the war?**

The war did not bring an end to bad feelings between the North and the South. A Northern army *occupied* the South for a few years. The Southerners did not like having Northern soldiers there. The Southerners were angry that their property had been destroyed and that they had lost the war. It would take many years for people on both sides to forgive each other.

President Lincoln Is Killed

Right after the war ended, President Lincoln was shot and killed. The president was in a theater in Washington watching a play when a Marylander named John Wilkes Booth *assassinated* him. Booth hated Lincoln and blamed him for the Civil War.

After the shooting, Booth ran out of the theater. He rode on horseback to Charles County, Maryland, and crossed the Potomac River into Virginia. There, Booth and another man trapped themselves in a barn. When officials ordered the men to come out of the barn, the man Booth was with did, but Booth refused. Officials set the barn on fire. Booth died in the blaze.

Many cities in the South had been destroyed in the Civil War. **What destruction is shown in this picture of Richmond, Virginia?**

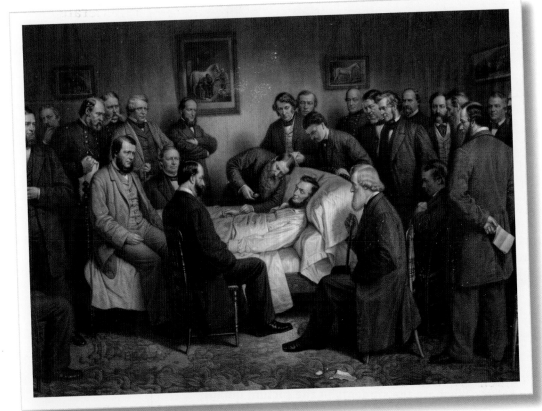

After President Lincoln was shot, he was taken to a home across the street from the theater, where he died a few hours later. **What do you think the doctor leaning over Lincoln's bed is doing?**

African Americans After the War

African Americans across the United States celebrated the end of slavery. However, former slaves still faced difficult challenges. In Maryland and across the South, many blacks left their homes in search of a new life. They had to find work. They had to provide their own food and shelter. They were very poor. Many could not read or write. Freedom did not mean the end of the problems.

Some white Marylanders did not want to treat African Americans as equals. Even though slavery was over, laws were not fair for black people. Blacks were not allowed to vote. Public schools did not allow black children to attend. It was hard for blacks to get good jobs.

After the Civil War, African Americans built schools like this one. Teachers, both black and white, worked hard to meet the needs of children who had not been allowed to go to school before. **What are the students in the picture doing?**

The U.S. government set up the Freedmen's Bureau to help former slaves. The bureau helped build schools and gave food, shelter, and medical care to people who were in need.

African Americans helped themselves, too. They opened schools, often in church buildings. People with homes took in the homeless. Others fed the hungry until they could find work. It was a difficult time.

Voting Rights for African Americans

African Americans said they should be allowed to vote. Some whites agreed. When the 15th Amendment to the U.S. Constitution became law five years after the Civil War ended, African American men gained the right to vote. Still, no women, black or white, were allowed to vote.

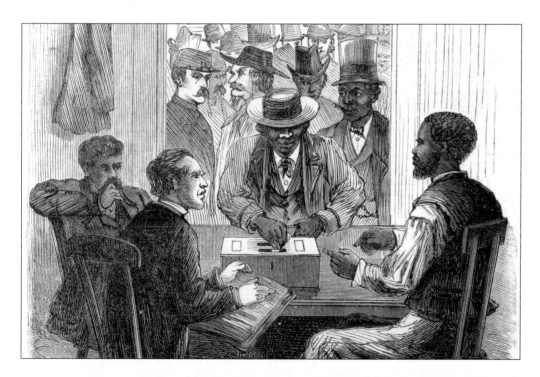

A few years after the Civil War, African American men got the right to vote. This scene shows a black man voting. **How do you think this man might have been feeling?**

③ KEY IDEA REVIEW

1. Why did the Southern states secede from the United States?
2. Were people in Maryland loyal to the Union or the Confederacy?
3. Describe one Civil War battle.
4. What did the Emancipation Proclamation do?

Go to the Source

Study a Letter from a Runaway Slave

This letter was written by a runaway slave to his wife in Maryland. The letter is typed below so that it is easier to read.

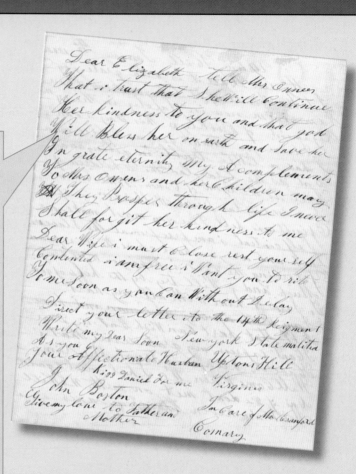

Dear Elizabeth tell Mrs Owens
That i trust that she will continue
Her kindness to you and that god
Will Bless her on earth and save her
In grate eternity my Acompelements
To Mrs Owens and her children may
They Prosper through life I never
Shall forgit her kindness to me
Dear Wife i must close rest yourself
Contented i am free i Want you to rite
To me soon as you can Without Delay
Direct your letter to the 14th Regiment
New york State malitia Upton Hill Virginia
In Care of Mr Cranford Cornary
Write my Dear Soon As you can
Your affectionate Husban John Boston
Kiss Daniel For me
Give my love to Father and Mother

LOOK	THINK	DECIDE
What do you notice about the spelling and punctuation of this letter written by a runaway slave?	What do the grammar and spelling mistakes in this letter tell you about the slave's education?	According to this letter, do you think that this runaway slave ever regretted his decision to run away or was he happier being free? List details from the letter to support your answer.

Chapter Review 7

Spotlighting Geography

Union, Confederate, and Border States

This is a map of America at the time of the Civil War.

1. How many slave states are shown on the map?
2. How many free states and territories are shown on the map?
3. List the states that bordered Maryland and what types of states they were.

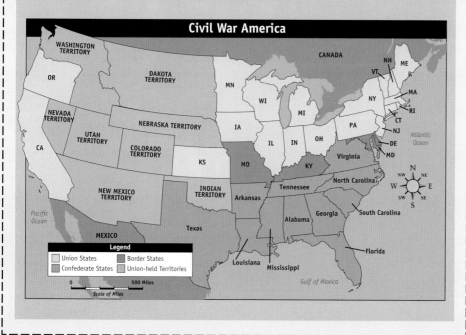

Civil War America

WASHINGTON TERRITORY

OR

NEVADA TERRITORY

CA

UTAH TERRITORY

DAKOTA TERRITORY

NEBRASKA TERRITORY

COLORADO TERRITORY

KS

NEW MEXICO TERRITORY

INDIAN TERRITORY

MEXICO

Texas

MN

WI

IA

IL

MO

IN

OH

KY

MI

PA

NY

VT

NH

ME

MA

RI

CT

NJ

DE

MD

Virginia

North Carolina

Tennessee

Arkansas

Mississippi

Alabama

Georgia

South Carolina

Louisiana

Florida

CANADA

Atlantic Ocean

Pacific Ocean

Gulf of Mexico

N S E W NW NE SW SE

Legend
- Union States
- Confederate States
- Border States
- Union-held Territories

0   500 Miles
Scale of Miles

Reviewing What You Read

1. What were the names of the two sides fighting in the Civil War?
2. What was a "slave" state?
3. Describe Maryland's point of view on slavery in your own words.
4. Why is the Emancipation Proclamation a significant document in our history?
5. Think of a person today who fights for what he or she believes in. Compare and contrast this person with an abolitionist from the mid-1800s.
6. Describe what the United States might be like today if the Civil War had never happened.

Becoming a Better Reader

Read a Nonfiction Book

Many groups of people were affected by the Civil War. What did children during the Civil War think? Read the book *The Children's Civil War*, by James Marten. Read the diaries and letters and look at the drawings from children on both sides of the conflict. Record your thoughts about and reactions to these children's lives.

A New Century

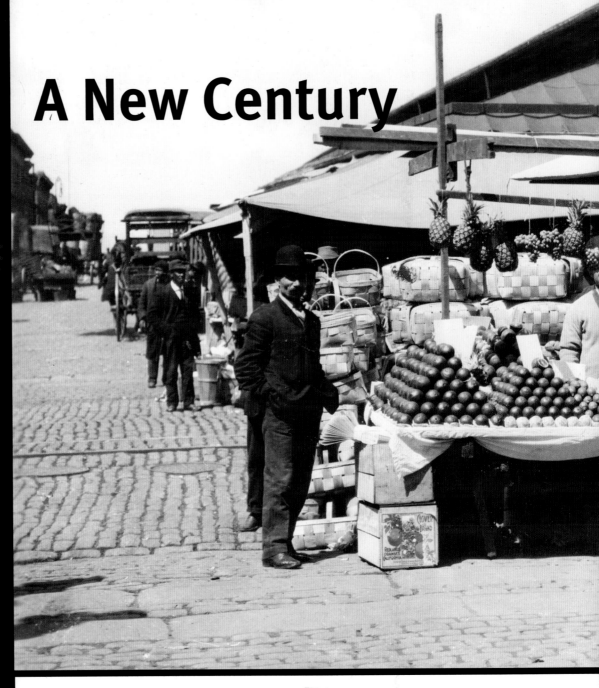

What's the Big Idea?

New industries, new inventions, new people, and new ideas changed the United States and Maryland in the early 20th century.

At the beginning of the 20th century, people looked to the future with great hope. They enjoyed many activities that we do today, such as shopping. **How was shopping at this Baltimore market, where fruit and flowers were sold, similar to shopping at a farmers market today?**

Timeline of Events

1870

1880

1876
Alexander Graham Bell invents the telephone.

1876
The Johns Hopkins University is founded.

1870–1910
Many industries start in Maryland.

Chapter 8

The beginning of the 20th century was a time of change in America and Maryland. Americans were building a new industrial society. They were improving roads and transportation. New inventions like the telephone, electric trolley, and machines powered by electricity made life easier.

Maryland and all of America also had problems. Many people had little money. Laws did not treat everyone equally. Workers, African Americans, and women fought for rights. People tried to make life better for their families.

1880–1910
New immigrants come to Maryland.

1893
The first gasoline-powered automobiles are invented.

1904
Downtown Baltimore is destroyed by fire.

1909
Baltimore builds a sewer system.

1890

1900

1910

1890s–1910s
Progressives pass laws.

1890s
Electric trolleys begin to be used in Maryland.

KEY IDEA

New jobs and a growing population changed life in Maryland.

WORDS TO UNDERSTAND

ghetto
mass production
migrant
process
quantity
recruit
refrigerate

A New America

As you read in the last two chapters, many important changes took place in Maryland during the 1800s. The state changed even more during the early 1900s.

New factories and the invention of new machines marked the rapid growth of the Industrial Revolution in America and in Maryland. Industry became more and more important to America's economy. Industries processed raw materials and made goods from those raw materials. To *process* means to go through a series of steps to prepare something.

Maryland's natural resources provided the materials that made industries successful. Soil, water, and minerals were resources people used to make a living.

Maryland cities and towns were becoming more industrial. **What clues in this picture of Ellicotts Mills indicate that the town was becoming more industrial?**

The Industrial Revolution in Maryland

As the 20th century began, Maryland cities grew larger than ever before. People moved to cities where industries offered jobs. Machines had been invented that could make things faster than people could by hand. Marylanders were building new industries, new streets, new stores, and new houses.

The 20th century means the 1900s.

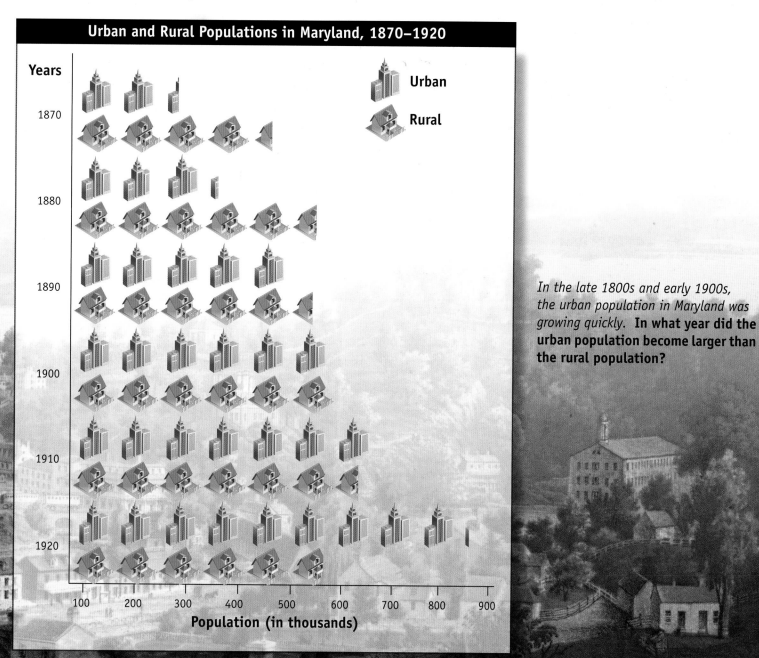

In the late 1800s and early 1900s, the urban population in Maryland was growing quickly. **In what year did the urban population become larger than the rural population?**

More and More Factories

Baltimore led the Industrial Revolution in Maryland. More and more factories were built in cities like Cumberland, Hagerstown, Frederick, and Salisbury. Factories were also built in smaller towns all across Maryland. People left their farms to work in factories. Some people moved to Maryland from other states and other countries to work in the factories.

Factories in Maryland processed food. They turned grain into flour. They canned fruits and vegetables. They canned oysters from the Chesapeake Bay. Local factories made clothing and hats. Soon, people realized the process of making large *quantities*, or amounts, was cheaper and easier than making products one at a time. This was called *mass production*.

The Industrial Revolution—Good and Bad

So much production made our country rich and strong. There were more goods available at lower prices. But there were problems, too. Some people, including children, worked long hours in unsafe factories. Workers did not earn much money.

Sometimes adults and children were hurt by machines. Companies said they were not responsible for the accidents. Workers often lost their jobs when they got hurt because they could no longer do as much work. Without jobs, families had no money to buy food or pay rent.

Young boys and girls worked in factories. **What types of work were the children in these pictures doing?**

Mass Production

Companies started to make many goods at once, instead of one at a time, using mass production. Let's see how it works.

If your mother sews a shirt at home, she cuts out the front, back, sleeves, and collar from a pattern. One by one, she sews the pieces together. Then she adds the buttons.

If shirts are mass-produced, one machine cuts out all the fronts. Another machine cuts out all the backs, sleeves, and collars. Another sews all the backs and fronts together. Another sews on all the sleeves. Finally, the last machine sews on all the buttons.

Mass production is fast! Since more shirts can be made in the same amount of time, each shirt can be sold for a lower price.

Linking the Present to the Past

Most of our goods today are mass-produced just as they were in the early 20th century. What goods do you use today that are mass-produced?

Farm Work

There were still many farm families in the early 1900s. Farmers grew grains, vegetables, and fruits. They also raised animals for dairy products and meat.

People who owned large farms often hired workers to help with the harvest. Some of these laborers were called *migrant* workers. They moved, or migrated, from farm to farm as different crops became ready to harvest. Some of the migrant workers were Americans, both black and white, and some were immigrants from other countries.

Migrant families started work as early as 4:30 in the morning. Even the children got up early to work in the fields. Some of the work they did was what slaves had done before the Civil War. Unlike slaves, migrant workers were paid, though not very much.

Large canneries and modern transportation allowed farm products to be sold over a wide area. Large farms produced more food for this larger market.

Migrant families, like this family from Poland, worked very hard to harvest crops. **What does this photo tell you about who was responsible for doing the farmwork?**

Jobs on the Water

Watermen harvested oysters, clams, and fish from the Chesapeake Bay and nearby rivers. Railroad cars that were *refrigerated* kept food cold and made it possible to ship seafood all across the country. Maryland became famous for its seafood.

John Crisfield started a company that built a railroad to carry the seafood from Maryland to Philadelphia and New York. The town of Crisfield is named after him. Twenty to thirty railroad cars full of oysters left Crisfield every day. Crisfield became the center of the oyster-processing industry. A canning process that used steam allowed the oysters to be preserved and shipped all the way to California.

Because oysters brought a high price in the market, many watermen competed to get the most oysters. Sometimes they harvested oysters from places that were off limits.

Watermen harvested seafood. **Can you describe what each of the three men in this drawing is doing?**

Isaac Myers
1835–1891

Shipbuilding and ship repair were important industries in Baltimore. Isaac Myers owned a shipyard called the Chesapeake Marine Railway and Dry Dock Company. Myers was an important leader in the African American community in Baltimore.

One reason Myers opened his business was because many businesses that whites owned refused to hire African American workers. Myers employed more than 300 black workers. He paid them $3 a day, a good wage for that time.

Myers, who had grown up in Baltimore, was also involved in other work. He helped other African Americans start businesses of their own. He helped produce a local newspaper. He was active in the Republican Party. Most African Americans at this time belonged to the Republican Party because President Abraham Lincoln, a Republican, had ended slavery.

Myers did a lot of volunteer work for his church and for many civic organizations. He gave his time and money to help make life better for the people of his community.

Men and boys did dangerous coal-mining work. **From looking at this picture, can you list some of the tools that they used to do their job?**

Linking the Present to the Past

Today, miners use modern equipment and computers, but the job is still dangerous. Sometimes mines cave in, and miners can get sick from breathing in too much dust.

Jobs in the Mines

Maryland had many valuable natural resources. Iron, copper, and tin were found in Maryland. Coal was also a very important resource from our state. Families used it to heat their homes and cook. Industries burned coal to boil water, which made steam that powered the engines of steamboats, trains, and machines.

Coal was not easy to get to. Men and boys worked deep in underground mines, digging out the coal by hand. It was a very dangerous job because sometimes the ground caved in around them. The miners also breathed in the coal dust, which caused lung diseases.

Once coal was mined, companies used the railroads to move the coal to industrial plants across the state. Coal was also used to make steel. Steel was used to make parts for ships and railroad tracks. Countries around the world bought tracks made in Maryland. Maryland's largest steel plant was at Sparrows Point.

New Immigrants

With all the new industries and growing cities, there were lots of jobs. Immigrants from other countries came to work in American industries. Industries *recruited* workers from other countries. They convinced them to come to America to work. Immigrants wanted to move to America to have a better life and to enjoy more freedoms. Their work helped build our nation's industrial strength.

America, "Land of Opportunity"

Immigrants looked to America as a "land of opportunity." They hoped to find religious and political freedom here. They hoped to find good jobs, safe homes, and plenty of food to eat. They hoped life would be better for their children in America.

Immigrants from Different Countries

Immigrants came to America from many different countries. Most of the immigrants who came to Maryland during this time were from Europe. They came from England, Ireland, and Germany, as they had for many years. New immigrants also came from southern and eastern Europe. Italians were one of the largest groups. Crops had failed in Italy and people did not have much to eat. Families left countries like Poland and Greece because they felt their governments treated them unfairly. Some immigrants also came from the West Indies and even as far away as China.

Jewish people left Russia and Poland because they were treated badly there. They were not allowed to own land. They were not allowed to go to universities or serve in the army. Often Jews were forced to live together in small, crowded areas within cities called *ghettos*. Many of their homes and synagogues, or places of worship, were burned down. Some Jews came to the United States because our laws guaranteed freedom of religion and because they would be treated better.

Make Choices

Pretend you are moving to another country. You must travel like the immigrants did 100 years ago. You can't pack much. You will be sailing on a boat with hundreds of strangers. There is hardly room for you, let alone your things. You must carry everything with you.

You can take only those things that will fit into a grocery bag. What will you choose to take with you? Make a list of what you will bring. Explain why you chose each item.

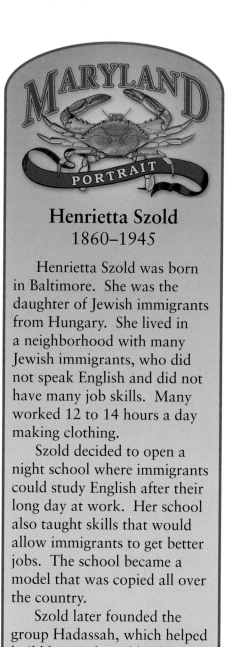

Henrietta Szold
1860–1945

Henrietta Szold was born in Baltimore. She was the daughter of Jewish immigrants from Hungary. She lived in a neighborhood with many Jewish immigrants, who did not speak English and did not have many job skills. Many worked 12 to 14 hours a day making clothing.

Szold decided to open a night school where immigrants could study English after their long day at work. Her school also taught skills that would allow immigrants to get better jobs. The school became a model that was copied all over the country.

Szold later founded the group Hadassah, which helped build hospitals and health clinics in Israel. In 2007, Szold was admitted to the National Women's Hall of Fame.

Journey to America

The journey to America was difficult. Poor conditions on the ships and rough seas caused many people to get sick. Some died. Many immigrants brought only what they could carry with them on the ship. They arrived in America with very few things, no clothes, and often no money.

"All of us poor people had to go down through a hole to the bottom of the ship. There was a big dark room down there with rows of wooden shelves all around where we were going to sleep—the Italian, the German, the Polish, the Swede, the French—every kind."

—Rosa Cristofero, Italy

"[There were] six of us kids . . . after two weeks and a bit seasick we unloaded . . . we got an eye exam. Some man came along. He gave us a box of food. . . . In the box there was a banana. We didn't know how to eat it. We'd never seen bananas. Finally somebody realized that and showed us."

—Nicholas Gerros, Greece

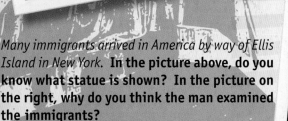

Many immigrants arrived in America by way of Ellis Island in New York. **In the picture above, do you know what statue is shown? In the picture on the right, why do you think the man examined the immigrants?**

Ships brought immigrants to Locust Point in Baltimore. **What do you think these immigrants were thinking about?**

Five Reasons People Came to America

1. To escape poverty and poor living conditions
2. To enjoy the freedoms of democracy
3. To escape war
4. To be free to practice their religion
5. To join other family members who had come earlier

From the Old World to the New World

1 KEY IDEA REVIEW

1. Explain the jobs people had in Maryland during this time and the problems they faced.
2. Why did immigrants come to America during this time?

KEY IDEA

New technologies changed the way people lived.

WORDS TO UNDERSTAND

generator
kerosene
sanitation
streetcar
suburb
technology

Ice was used to keep food stored in an icebox cold. **Can you list three things shown in this picture that people today no longer use?**

Inventions Change Life

People 150 years ago did not have the *technology* we have today. There were no televisions or computers. Most people did not have cars or telephones. They had never flown in an airplane. If you could travel back in time to the late 19th century, you would find that life was very different.

Machines That Use Electricity

In 1870, if you wanted to cook or heat your house, you had to light a stove filled with coal or wood. To get light, people filled lamps with an oil called *kerosene*. Today, all you do is turn a knob or flip a switch to get gas, light, or heat.

Electric generators were one of the most important new inventions of the 1900s. A *generator* is a machine that makes electricity. It changed the way people worked, played, and lived.

Streets and homes were lit with electric lights for the first time. Machines that used electricity were soon invented. People began buying electric washing machines, irons, stoves, refrigerators, and vacuum cleaners. *Streetcars* were powered by electric wires and ran on rails instead of being pulled by horses. Streetcars were also called electric trolleys.

Thomas Edison invented the light bulb.
Does this light bulb look like light bulbs today?

Telegraph and Telephone

The telegraph came into use in the 1840s. It allowed communication along electric wires using a series of signals called the Morse code.

Before 1870, there was still no way to talk with someone across town. You had to write them a letter or visit them in person. Alexander Graham Bell's invention, the telephone, made it easier for people to communicate. Soon, Marylanders could call from town to town and talk as we do on the telephone today.

What Do You Think?

Which inventions do you think are the greatest ever made? Explain why.

Alexander Graham Bell invented the telephone. **How is this early phone different from phones today?**

Fire in Baltimore!

In February 1904, a fire broke out in the Hurst Dry Goods Company in Baltimore. Then an explosion and high winds spread the fire all over the downtown area.

The fire burned for a day and a half. Freezing temperatures made it hard for firemen to fight the fire. Some of the water from their hoses turned to ice. Firemen from neighboring towns came to help, but many of their hoses were the wrong size to connect to Baltimore's fire hydrants. Before the fire was put out, over 1,500 buildings had burned. The heart of downtown Baltimore was destroyed. Thousands of people no longer had a place to work. Because the fire started on a Sunday, most people were not at work in the downtown area so they were not caught in the fire.

Baltimore took advantage of the tragedy to build a more modern city. The city put in a modern sewer system, built wider streets, and also enlarged the fire department.

The Baltimore fire destroyed much of the downtown area. **What damage do you see in this picture?**

215

People took tours of the new sewers before they were put in use. **Would you dress up like these men to take a tour of a sewer?**

Sewer System

Most people went to a well or spring to get water 150 years ago. This took a lot of time. Sometimes the water was polluted. People's toilets drained straight into the ground.

Cumberland, for example, got its drinking water from the Potomac River. The city also drained its waste water into the same river. Thousands of people got a disease called typhoid fever every year from drinking the unhealthy water.

Around 1900, Marylanders began working to improve *sanitation*. Baltimore began to pump water from the Gunpowder River. This brought cleaner drinking water to the city. People who could afford it had water pumped directly into their houses. They just turned on their faucets and water came out.

Baltimore built a sewer system to collect waste water. The sewers carried the dirty water to a treatment plant where it was cleaned. Soon, smaller cities were building their own sewer systems and water treatment plants.

Life In and Near Cities

Cities began to grow so large that people could no longer walk from one place to another. People began riding in open buses pulled by horses to get around. Once a city got electricity, streetcars replaced the horse-drawn buses.

Automobiles

Wealthy people began buying automobiles at the beginning of the 1900s. At first, cars were used mainly for fun because they were not very dependable. It was common for cars to get several flat tires in one day. Many roads were still not paved, so cars got stuck in the mud often.

Streetcar Suburbs

Streets and trolley lines began to branch out from cities like spokes on a wheel. People began to live along the "spokes" because they could get to work easily. People also began to build **suburbs**, or neighborhoods just outside the downtown area. Sometimes people called these neighborhoods streetcar suburbs.

Trolley lines connected suburbs to a city. **Can you point out the city and suburbs in this drawing?**

Sunday in the Park

As Maryland's roadways and cities grew, people worried there would soon be no more open spaces. People set aside large areas of land with trees, lakes, and nice grassy places for picnics. On Sundays, families often took a trolley car to a park to spend the day. Druid Hill Park in Baltimore is shown below.

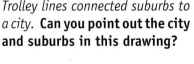

2 KEY IDEA REVIEW

1. How did new technologies change the way people lived?
2. Describe three new inventions.

KEY IDEA

Problems in the new century inspired people to come up with ideas to make life better.

WORDS TO UNDERSTAND

labor union
luxury
middle class
philanthropist
politics
segregate

This painting shows rich people watching a golf game at the Chevy Chase Club. Some poor families lived in one-room shacks in Anne Arundel County. **How do you think the daily lives of poor people were different from rich people?**

Problems in the New Century

People in the early 20th century faced problems. There were many poor people who struggled to survive. Their children often had to work long hours in factories instead of going to school. Life was not always fair for all people.

The Rich and the Poor

There were some wealthy families in Maryland during this time. They had made a lot of money in business and industry. Rich families lived in big houses, wore fine clothes, and had servants. They were the first to have running water, electricity, and cars.

There were many more poor families than rich families. In cities, poor families often lived in buildings that had no running water. They had to go outside to get water and to use the bathroom. In places where there was running water, several families shared a bathroom and a kitchen.

Many families were not rich or poor. They had homes and enough to eat, but they did not have **luxuries** like the wealthy. They worked hard to pay for food, water, clothes, and shelter. These people who were not rich or poor were **middle class**.

Schools 100 Years Ago

By 1900, every county in Maryland had public schools. In small towns, most schools had only one or two rooms.

Many boys and girls worked instead of going to school. They had jobs in factories or mines or on farms. Their families needed them to work to make money for the family. No laws required children to go to school, so many poor children never even learned to read.

Schools across the state were *segregated*, which meant white children and black children had to go to different schools. In many places, white schools got the newest buildings, books, and equipment. Schools for black children often got what was left over.

Many immigrant families did not speak English when they first came to the United States. It was hard for children to learn when they could not understand what their teachers were saying. Many immigrant children did not go to school at all.

African American children attended this segregated public school in Annapolis. **What are the students in this picture doing?**

Working to Make Things Better

America and Maryland faced a lot of problems during this time. Many men and women wanted to make life better. One way they tried to change things was by becoming involved in *politics*, activities related to running the government and making laws.

These men and women formed a political group called the Progressives. In the early 1900s, the Progressives passed laws requiring factories to be safer. They helped get new laws passed that required companies to pay their workers more. Other laws said that children could not work in factories and mines. These laws required children to go to school. Getting an education was important so children could get better jobs once they grew up.

Progressives held big meetings like this one in Illinois. **Did mostly men or women attend this meeting?**

African American men got the right to vote after the Civil War. **Do you think the method of voting shown in this picture gave voters privacy?**

The Power of Voting

As you read in the last chapter, African American men got the right to vote soon after the Civil War. In Annapolis, Baltimore, and Cambridge, black men were elected to city councils. They could now look out for the needs of people in their communities.

Immigrants understood that it was very important to get involved in their communities. Many became American citizens so they could vote and take part in political activities. Soon, Irish, Italian, and Polish immigrants held government jobs. They used their voices to help make new laws.

Most Progressives wanted women to be able to vote, too. They fought hard to change the voting laws. However, many men and some women did not want women to vote. They thought women did not know enough to vote. Women finally got the right to vote in 1920, which you will read about in the next chapter.

Labor Unions

Workers were another group of people who got together to help make life better. They formed ***labor unions*** to protect themselves and their rights. Labor unions demanded that companies pay workers more and make working conditions safer. Union leaders talked to government leaders and helped convince them to vote for these changes.

Wealthy people called *philanthropists* wanted to help improve people's lives and make our state a better place to live. They gave money to build hospitals, universities, libraries, and museums.

Enoch Pratt, a Baltimore merchant, gave the city money to open a free library. He said the library's books were "for all, rich or poor, without distinction of race or color."

William Jackson, a business leader in Salisbury, gave money to build a new and modern hospital. Today, this is called the Peninsula Regional Medical Center. It still serves people of the Eastern Shore.

The citizens of Frederick collected money to build a public park around the county courthouse. Benjamin Newcomer, of Hagerstown, gave money to open the Washington County Free Library.

Wiley Bates gave money to help open a high school for African American students in Anne Arundel County.

Volunteering

A lot of people volunteered their time and talents to make life better. Women in Allegany County opened a soup kitchen to feed the poor. Men and women opened settlement houses that taught immigrants and poor people skills like cooking and sewing, as well as how to speak English, so they could better their lives.

African American women and white women formed clubs. The clubs helped clean up the streets. They opened kindergartens and nurseries, where working mothers could take their children. Club members fought to make water and milk safe to drink. These women made a big difference in the lives of Marylanders.

Linking the Present to the Past

Volunteers did many things to make people's lives better in the 1900s. What kinds of things do volunteers in Maryland do today?

Many libraries at this time only allowed white people. **Was this Baltimore library, which Enoch Pratt gave money to build, segregated?**

German *submarines*, a type of ship that can travel under the water, started sinking American ships carrying these supplies. The United States declared war against Germany and its allies after Germany refused to stop the attacks. Soon, soldiers from Maryland were in Europe fighting.

Maryland During the War

Back home in Maryland, people made sacrifices to help the war effort. They had "heatless" Mondays, "meatless" Tuesdays, and "wheatless" Wednesdays to save resources. Women's clubs made bandages for hospitals that treated soldiers. Families grew their own food at home in "victory gardens." People did what they could to help support the war effort.

Soldiers from all over the country trained in Maryland. Camp Meade, now called Fort Meade, trained soldiers. It was built in Anne Arundel County because many railroad lines passed through the area. Trains made it easy for soldiers to get to the camp.

When men went to war, they left their jobs, but that work still had to be done. Many women left their homes to go to work. Women took jobs that men had done in factories, offices, and stores. They worked as telephone operators and on streetcars and railroads.

Maryland factories were busy making guns, tanks, ships, and other goods for the war. The Bethlehem Steel Company at Sparrows Point produced a lot of steel used for wartime supplies. Also, another important Maryland industry was the Baltimore Drydock and Shipping Company. People moved to cities to work in the war industries. Many people from southern states, both whites and blacks, came to work in Maryland.

Posters urged everyone to help in the war effort. **What does Uncle Sam—in his red, white, and blue—stand for?**

Girl Scouts collected peach pits for the war effort. The pits were turned into charcoal that was used in soldiers' gas masks to filter out poisonous gas. **What does the Girl Scouts' sign say?**

People around the country celebrated the end of World War I. **How did people in New York City show their patriotism?**

The War Ends

On the 11th hour of the 11th day of the 11th month of 1918, all fighting on the battlefields of Europe stopped. The news that the war was over arrived in America by telegraph.

Everyone in Maryland and across the nation celebrated. Towns held parades to honor soldiers. Troops marched through the streets as people cheered. Today, we celebrate November 11 as Veterans Day, in honor of all American veterans. *Veterans* are the men and women who served in the military.

Problems After the War

By the end of World War I, life had changed for many Americans. A lot of people did not return to the way of life they had before the war. Many men had been killed or injured. Women continued working outside the home. Most people who had moved to cities did not go back to rural areas.

When the war ended, factories making war supplies closed down. For a while, there were not enough jobs for all the soldiers returning to America. Many women who had worked in factories and at other jobs lost those jobs to veterans who were returning home. Many soldiers wanted to start a family and buy a home. There were not enough homes. People became angry.

The Great Migration

Thousands of African Americans moved from farms and towns in the South to cities in the North. They left the South for many reasons. Southern states did not protect blacks' political rights. Many blacks were prevented from voting. Some whites used violence to keep blacks from getting good jobs and nice homes. It was hard for blacks to get a good education. The South was also still segregated, or separated, based on race.

In the North, African Americans could vote. Jobs in industry paid better. Schools were better. Public places like parks and libraries were not segregated. Since many blacks left the rural South for cities of the North, this movement was called the Great Migration. Moving from one place to another is called a *migration*.

Many African Americans left their homes in the South to migrate north. **How do you think this man felt about leaving his home?**

Ku Klux Klan

A group called the Ku Klux Klan (KKK) said that African Americans, Catholics, Jews, and immigrants were the cause of America's problems.

The KKK said blacks had too many rights. Angry mobs set fire to the homes of black families. Sometimes they killed blacks.

The KKK attacked Catholics and Jews because of their religion. The Klan believed immigrant workers were taking jobs away from people who had been born in America, so they attacked them.

KKK members wore white robes with hoods that covered their faces. They wanted to scare people.

A few Marylanders joined the KKK. The Klan held marches in several Maryland cities. However, most people in Maryland and across the country thought the Klan was very un-American because it did not believe in the ideas written in our Constitution. They did not like the bad things the group did. Maryland passed a law against parades of masked men to stop KKK marches.

The KKK blamed problems in our country on blacks, Catholics, Jews, and immigrants. **What do you think was the purpose of KKK rallies like this one?**

The Roaring Twenties

A few years after World War I ended, new industries made new jobs for people. Men and women went to work building radios, sewing machines, cars, railroad cars, airplanes, and many other products. People began to earn more money than they had before the war. This period was called the Roaring Twenties because many people were so prosperous and because so many people set out to have a good time. To be **prosperous** means to be successful.

Families in small towns got electricity for the first time. New machines were making life easier in many ways. Now families could clean with electric vacuum cleaners, wash clothes in electric washing machines, and keep food in electric refrigerators.

Some people wanted to forget about the war and just have fun. A new type of music called jazz was popular. So were lively dances, such as the Charleston. Musicians, artists, and writers tried out wonderful new styles. Radio became popular. Marylanders were part of this exciting new culture.

Cars

Many families bought their first car in the 1920s. Henry Ford used an assembly line to make cars for a low cost.

The U.S. government built new roads all across the country. The cars used a lot of gasoline, so oil companies became rich and powerful. There were also fewer horses on the streets, which kept streets cleaner.

Cars provided people with a lot of freedom. They could travel wherever they wanted to. Cars also made it easier for people to travel longer distances to work. People began to build houses in suburbs away from the cities.

New styles of clothes and new dances were part of the Roaring Twenties. **Do the people shown on this magazine cover look like they are worrying about the world's problems or enjoying a good time?**

The Harlem Renaissance was a movement that celebrated African American culture. **What were the people in this club doing?**

The Harlem Renaissance

In the big cities, there were many African American musicians, writers, and artists. These men and women explored and celebrated the lives and culture of African Americans. They were part of a movement called the Harlem Renaissance. This was a period of great activity in the arts. Harlem, a neighborhood in New York City, was the center of the movement. Artists and musicians also lived and worked in Baltimore and other cities across the country.

Eubie Blake and Cab Calloway were famous jazz musicians from Maryland. People traveled from all over Maryland to Baltimore and Washington, D.C., when they performed.

Sports

Americans enjoyed watching and playing sports. Many people in Maryland cheered for professional sports teams. Baseball was especially popular. The great baseball player Babe Ruth got his start with the Baltimore Orioles. School teams were formed.

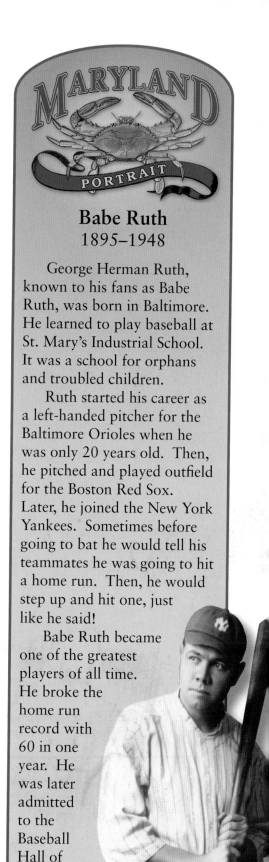

MARYLAND PORTRAIT

Babe Ruth
1895–1948

George Herman Ruth, known to his fans as Babe Ruth, was born in Baltimore. He learned to play baseball at St. Mary's Industrial School. It was a school for orphans and troubled children.

Ruth started his career as a left-handed pitcher for the Baltimore Orioles when he was only 20 years old. Then, he pitched and played outfield for the Boston Red Sox. Later, he joined the New York Yankees. Sometimes before going to bat he would tell his teammates he was going to hit a home run. Then, he would step up and hit one, just like he said!

Babe Ruth became one of the greatest players of all time. He broke the home run record with 60 in one year. He was later admitted to the Baseball Hall of Fame.

Women Win the Right to Vote

Women had been working to gain the right to vote for a long time. A woman in colonial Maryland named Margaret Brent asked for the right to vote, but she did not get it. Some women hoped that when African American men got the right to vote in 1870 that women would also get that right. But they did not.

Women who fought for the right to vote called themselves suffragists. *Suffrage* means the right to vote. Suffragists held marches, sang songs, and gave speeches about why women should be allowed to vote. Maryland, like all states, had suffrage groups. Women sent letters and telegrams to government officials.

Finally, the 19th Amendment was added to the U.S. Constitution. It gave every adult woman the right to vote. Mary Risteau, of Harford County, was elected the first woman member of the Maryland House of Delegates.

VOTES FOR WOMEN.

For the work of a day.
For the taxes we pay.
For the Laws we obey.
We want something to say.

Suffragists fought for women's right to vote. **What arguments does this drawing use to further the suffragists' cause?**

Help us to win the vote

Suffragists wanted women to have the right to vote. **What does this woman's sign say?**

Although Prohibition was not strongly enforced in Maryland, it was in other states. **What do you think the men in this picture were dumping down the sewer?**

Prohibition

The 1920s was a decade with a lot of crime and violence. One reason was Prohibition. The government *prohibited*, or forbade, people from making and selling alcoholic drinks.

People who still wanted to drink went to "speakeasies," secret clubs where they could buy alcohol. "Bootlegging," or the making and selling of alcohol illegally, became big business. Criminals, who were often violent, took over the selling of illegal alcohol. Sometimes they murdered people who bought alcohol from other people.

The government in Maryland did not think Prohibition was a good idea and did not support it very much. Prohibition did not last long. Alcohol was soon made legal again.

1 KEY IDEA REVIEW

1. What contributions did people at home make to support the war effort?
2. Describe two ways life changed for people following World War I.

KEY IDEA

The United States experienced a serious depression. The government stepped in to fix the problems.

WORDS TO UNDERSTAND

agency
depression
discrimination
employment
lay off
poverty
unemployed

The Great Depression

During the 1930s, our country faced a serious *depression*. Many banks failed, and people lost all of their savings. Thousands of people during the 1930s lost their jobs. They wanted to work, but they couldn't find *employment*. Without jobs, they couldn't buy things. They stopped buying new homes. They couldn't afford to buy radios, cars, or even clothes.

Since fewer people were buying things, people working in the factories lost their jobs. People who built homes lost their jobs, too. Then, even more people couldn't buy things. It seemed the cycle would never end.

The depression of the 1930s was the worst depression the United States has ever experienced. That is why it was called the Great Depression.

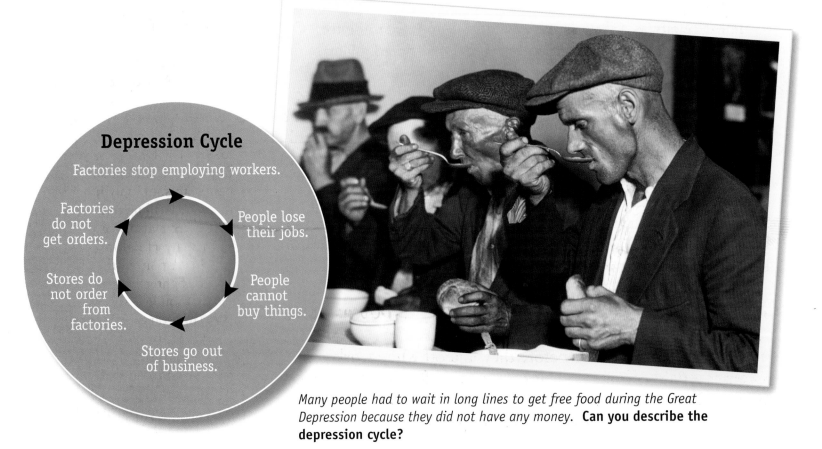

Depression Cycle

Factories stop employing workers.

Factories do not get orders.

People lose their jobs.

Stores do not order from factories.

People cannot buy things.

Stores go out of business.

Many people had to wait in long lines to get free food during the Great Depression because they did not have any money. **Can you describe the depression cycle?**

Many people had a hard time during the Depression making enough money to take care of their families. **What clues in this picture suggest that this woman, who was a migrant worker, and her children were suffering?**

Struggling to Survive

In every city in Maryland, many families lived in *poverty*. People stood in long lines to get free soup and bread. Men sold apples on street corners to earn money. People mended old clothes again and again to try to make them last. They put cardboard in the bottoms of their shoes when the soles wore out.

People tried to help each other as much as they could. Local police and firefighters collected food and gave it to families who had no money.

For Americans who were already poor, life got much worse. Many families lost their homes. Soon there were homeless people everywhere. The homeless often lived along railroad tracks in shacks they built from scraps of wood or metal.

African Americans and Women During the Depression

During this troubled time, some companies *laid off*, or stopped employing, black workers before they laid off white workers. Often they laid off women before they laid off men. Many people protested this *discrimination*. They said it was wrong to favor one group—white men—above everybody else.

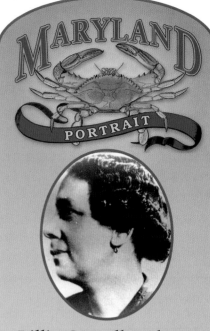

The New Deal

People began to wonder if the Depression would ever end. When Franklin Delano Roosevelt became president, he had a plan called the New Deal. The government started hundreds of projects that created thousands of jobs for Americans.

"I pledge you, I pledge myself, to a new deal for the American people."

—Franklin Roosevelt

President Roosevelt created many New Deal programs to help Americans and help the United States recover from the Depression. **Do you think all Americans agreed with Roosevelt's plan?**

New Government Agencies

As part of the New Deal, the government set up *agencies* to hire out-of-work, or *unemployed*, people. Because the names of these agencies were so long, people started calling them by their initials instead. There were so many agencies that some people called them "alphabet soup."

The Civilian Conservation Corps (CCC) put young men to work building parks, golf courses, playgrounds, and hiking trails.

The Works Progress Administration (WPA) put men and a few women to work building new schools, post offices, roads, and bridges. Artists were hired to paint large paintings on walls. Actors were hired to put on shows. Historians were hired to write local histories. Some historians wrote the stories of people who had been slaves.

The WPA put many people to work doing construction and other projects. **What was the message of this WPA poster?**

Chapter 9: Two World Wars and the Great Depression

The Farm Security Administration (FSA) helped farmers. FSA workers traveled to farms across Maryland and the nation, teaching modern ways of farming. They also gave out general health and safety information.

Thousands of people worked for the government during Roosevelt's New Deal. Some Americans were unhappy the government had grown so large. However, many people were happy to have jobs once again.

Greenbelt

Many of the new government agencies were located in Washington, D.C. Thousands of families began to move into Maryland, near the nation's capital, to work at the agencies. President Roosevelt approved the building of planned towns in order to create housing and jobs. One of these towns was Greenbelt, in Prince George's County, just 12 miles from Washington, D.C. City planners built a town center with a school, library, shops, and entertainment. Greenbelt was a model for many other planned communities.

Greenbelt, a planned suburb in Prince George's County, was part of one of the New Deal programs. **What does this advertisement for Greenbelt show pictures of?**

The FSA helped this farmer by lending him money to build a new well. **How do you think this farmer's life was similar to and different from the lives of farmers today?**

2 KEY IDEA REVIEW

1. Explain the cycle of depression.
2. How did President Roosevelt respond to the Great Depression?

KEY IDEA

The United States fought in World War II and afterwards became a world leader.

WORDS TO UNDERSTAND

atomic bomb
concentration camp
dictator
invade
patrol
ration

World War II began when Germany invaded Poland. **What does this picture of German soldiers tell you about their training?**

World War II

While Americans were struggling through the Great Depression, many people in other countries were also struggling. President Roosevelt helped America get through those difficult years. Not all countries were so lucky. Some countries did not have responsible leaders.

In some countries, dictators took over the government. A *dictator* is a ruler who has all the power over a country and its people. Germany and Italy both had dictators. The dictators stopped holding elections. They killed people who were against them. In Japan, the army took over the government.

The dictators took over many of their neighboring countries. The German army *invaded* Poland. England and France declared war on Germany for entering and attacking Poland. England and France formed an alliance with other countries to oppose Germany. They were called the Allies. World War II had started.

Japan joined Germany and Italy to form the Axis Powers. During the early years of the war, the United States helped the Allied Forces by sending them supplies. However, our country stayed out of the fighting.

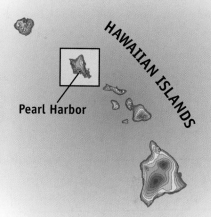

The Japanese attacked Pearl Harbor, sinking U.S. ships and killing many Americans. **Where is Pearl Harbor located?**

Attack on Pearl Harbor

On December 7, 1941, Japanese airplanes surprised Americans by dropping bombs on the U.S. Navy base at Pearl Harbor, Hawaii. The Japanese sank or severely damaged almost every U.S. ship. Bombs also destroyed American planes on airfields. More than 2,000 Americans were killed.

The next day, the United States declared war on Japan. In his speech to the nation, President Roosevelt said that Americans would never forget the date December 7, 1941, the day of the horrible bombing.

Once again, our country was at war. Americans were fighting against Japan, Germany, and Italy. Our allies included Great Britain, France, Russia, and China. This truly was a world war.

Many soldiers from Maryland served in World War II. **What type of transportation were these soldiers using for travel?**

The U.S. government created posters to encourage Americans to support the war effort. **What is the message of this poster?**

Marylanders Help the War Effort

After the attack on Pearl Harbor, thousands of Americans signed up to fight. Maryland sent over 240,000 men and women to serve in the war. Our soldiers and sailors fought in many places across the world, including Europe, Asia, Africa, and on ships in the Atlantic and Pacific Oceans.

Maryland also sent medical units to help soldiers fighting in the war. Doctors and nurses from Johns Hopkins, the University of Maryland, Provident Hospital, and many others took care of wounded and dying soldiers. Over 4,000 Marylanders died in World War II.

Guarding the Home Front

It was also important to protect America while U.S. soldiers were overseas. Guards were posted all along Maryland's beaches to watch for German ships and submarines. Just north of Ocean City, across the Delaware border, you can still see concrete towers where the guards stood watch.

Because modern airplanes could easily fly from Europe across the ocean to America, states along the Atlantic Coast feared an air attack by Germany. Families hung heavy black shades in their windows. If pilots could not see any lights, they would not know where to drop bombs. Local volunteers *patrolled*, or carefully passed through, every neighborhood to make sure people were following the blackout rules.

Many Americans made sacrifices to help the war effort. **What does this poster urge people to do?**

Rationing

To be sure Allied soldiers had everything they needed, the U.S. government put limits on what people at home could buy. It *rationed* goods, or gave people only certain amounts, to make sure there was enough for the troops. Each member of a family received stamps for goods like sugar, meat, butter, coffee, gas, and tires. The stamps were free, but people had to give them to shopkeepers when they bought the goods. People also had to pay for the goods. When the stamps ran out, the family had to wait until the next month to buy more items.

When goods became scarce, people borrowed or shared their stamps. Together, families could gather enough ingredients to bake a cake or enough gasoline to drive a long distance. As during World War I, families planted "victory gardens" to grow their own fruits and vegetables.

In order to buy goods during the war, people had to pay for the product plus the required number of ration coupons. **What was the price and number of ration coupons required to buy canned apple juice at this store?**

What Do You Think

Would you be willing to have less of something so other people could have some, too?

War Industries in Maryland

Maryland's industries made a big contribution to the war effort. The war created many jobs in factories where airplanes, tanks, guns, uniforms, and other supplies were made.

In Baltimore, Frederick, Hagerstown, Cumberland, and other cities across our state, factories built ships and airplanes. Workers at the Bethlehem Steel Fairchild Shipyards built 500 Victory and Liberty ships. The Glenn L. Martin Company supplied bombers to American forces and to our allies.

All these wartime industries ended the job problem in America and the Great Depression. In fact, because of the war, companies were always looking for workers. They hired women and African Americans, many of whom were not able to get factory jobs during the Great Depression.

Women Help at Home

To encourage women to take jobs in factories, the government came up with the idea of "Rosie the Riveter." A rivet is a bolt that holds two pieces of metal together. Posters showed Rosie in a blue work shirt and a red-and-white bandanna.

High wages and an opportunity to learn new skills were exciting to many women. Thousands went to work. Their work was very important to the war effort.

Many women went to work during World War II to help the war effort. **What is the message of this Rosie the Riveter poster?**

Chapter 9: Two World Wars and the Great Depression

THE HOLOCAUST

Adolf Hitler, the dictator of Germany, believed Germans were better than all other people. He said Germans should rule the whole world. Hitler hated many people who weren't Germans. He especially hated Jews. Hitler used his power to pass laws that took away the rights of Jewish people. All Jews had to wear an armband with a yellow star on it. If they did not wear it, they were arrested. At first, Hitler ordered Jews to live in certain neighborhoods. Then, he forced them to leave their homes altogether.

Soon, Hitler decided to kill all Jews. At gunpoint, soldiers forced Jews into railroad cars and sent them to concentration camps. Some Jews were hidden by neighbors and other people, but most could not escape Hitler's terror.

More than 12 million people died in the concentration camps. About 6 million of these were Jews. Others included disabled people, prisoners, and people from countries Hitler had invaded. At concentration camps, there was hardly anything to eat. The people were forced to do hard labor until they died. People who were too old, too young, or too weak to work were killed.

By the time Allied Forces found the remaining prisoners, many were so starved they were too sick to eat. Some died even after being freed. Entire towns and families were wiped out. Some survivors spent the rest of their lives looking for lost family and friends. Today, this tragedy is called the Holocaust.

Jews had to wear an armband with a yellow star on it. **How do you think this woman and other Jewish people felt about this?**

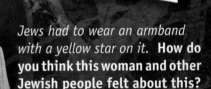

Prisoners at concentration camps suffered greatly, and many died. **What evidence do you see of suffering in this picture?**

245

The End of the War

The Allied Forces began winning the war. In Europe, Allied Forces were pushing towards Germany. Airplanes regularly dropped bombs on German factories, making it difficult for Germany to keep troops supplied.

Hitler soon realized the war was lost. He knew he would face terrible punishment if he were captured. Hitler killed himself. Soon after, the Germans surrendered to the Allied Forces. The war in Europe was over. In Maryland and across the United States, people celebrated V-E Day. V-E meant "Victory in Europe."

President Roosevelt died shortly before V-E Day. Roosevelt's vice president, Harry Truman, became president.

The Atomic Bomb

The war with Germany had ended, but there was still fierce fighting against Japan. Hundreds of soldiers were killed or wounded every day. Leaders in the United States had a hard decision to make. Should they risk more American lives, or should they drop the atomic bomb and end the war? The *atomic bomb* was a new bomb that was the most powerful that had ever been created.

When the United States dropped the atomic bomb on Hiroshima, Japan, a violent explosion destroyed much of the city and killed thousands of people. **What damage do you see in the bottom picture?**

MARYLAND SOCIAL STUDIES SKILLS AND PROCESSES

SKILLS

Write and Research a Question

Choose one of the following topics or another topic from Lesson 3. Think of a question about that topic that was NOT already answered in your reading. Research books, encyclopedias, or the Internet to find the answer to your question. Write a paragraph about your findings.

- The attack on Pearl Harbor
- The Holocaust
- Women's roles in World War II
- The atomic bomb

President Harry Truman asked the Japanese to surrender. After Japan refused, Truman surprised the world. He dropped the first atomic bomb on Hiroshima, Japan. Still, the Japanese refused to surrender.

Three days later, the United States dropped another atomic bomb on the Japanese city of Nagasaki. The destruction and loss of life in the two cities were immense. After the second blast, Japan surrendered. People in Maryland and around the world celebrated V-J Day. V-J Day meant "Victory in Japan."

Peace

After years of fighting and millions of deaths, the war was over. People in Maryland and across the country celebrated. World War II was a major event in American history. America was luckier than most countries because there had been no fighting here on our own land. Our farms could still produce food. Our factories could still make goods. People's homes had not been destroyed.

Many nations looked to the United States to help them rebuild after the war. The United States was now a world leader. The United States had more responsibilities than ever before because our country was the strongest in the world.

Soldiers and other Americans celebrated the end of World War II in Europe. **What two events does this man's sign mention?**

③ KEY IDEA REVIEW

1. What event caused the United States to enter World War II?
2. How did Marylanders help in World War II?
3. What did America do to end World War II?

Go to the Source

Study a Photo from a Women's Suffrage Newspaper

Edith Houghton Hooker started the *Maryland Suffrage News*. The newspaper printed articles on suffrage. The paper helped women feel connected with like-minded women throughout Maryland. This photo was printed on the front page of the May 29, 1915, edition of the paper.

LOOK	THINK	DECIDE
What do you see in this picture that tells you it was taken long ago?	Why do you think this picture was on the cover of the *Maryland Suffrage News*?	If you would have been alive at this time, would you have supported women's suffrage? Explain why or why not.

Spotlighting Geography

Map World War II

Use a reference book like an encyclopedia or the Internet to do research on World War II. Make a list of all the countries that were involved in this world war. Next, organize the countries into two columns: one for the Allied Powers and one for the Axis Powers. Lastly, locate these countries on a map or globe.

Becoming a Better Reader

Recognize Point of View

You may have heard people say that everyone is entitled to his or her opinion. Good readers recognize how opinions are formed based on a person's point of view. Every person has a different point of view. As you learned in Chapter 1, a point of view is the way someone thinks about something. People's points of view are affected by where they live, how they were raised, their education, and many other factors. Choose an idea from this chapter that people had different opinions about. Write a couple of sentences about the idea from two different points of view. Some examples of topics you might choose to write about include whether America should have entered World War I, whether America's decisions to drop the atomic bombs were right or wrong, or whether women should be allowed to vote.

Reviewing What You Read

1. What sacrifices did Maryland make to help the World War I war effort?
2. When did World War I end?
3. Describe what it means to be neutral.
4. Why was women's suffrage significant in our history?
5. How did life during the Great Depression compare or contrast with life today?
6. What would life have been like if President Roosevelt had not created the New Deal?

Modern Maryland

What's the Big Idea?

After World War II, soldiers returned home and started families. Our country became involved in several more wars. Many Americans also fought for equal rights for all people.

The Maryland State Fair is held every year in Timonium. **What is there to do at this fair?**

Timeline of Events

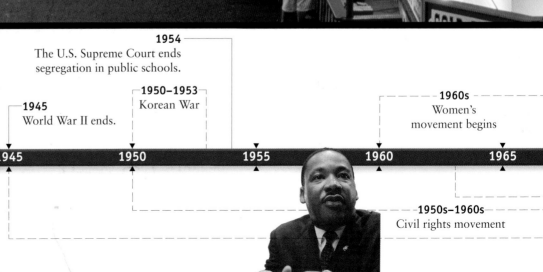

1945
World War II ends.

1950–1953
Korean War

1954
The U.S. Supreme Court ends segregation in public schools.

1960s
Women's movement begins

1950s–1960s
Civil rights movement

1945   1950   1955   1960   1965

Chapter 10

After World War II, Maryland experienced great growth and change.

The post war years were difficult in many ways. The United States fought in several wars. Many people still did not have equal rights. Many groups led protests to get equal rights.

Today, people are continuing to speak out for what they think is right. People want to make sure that our country and state are safe, that our rights are upheld, and that our environment is protected.

1976
The Washington Metro links Maryland suburbs to downtown Washington, D.C.

2001
- Terrorists attack the United States.
- War in Afghanistan begins.

| 1975 | 1980 | 1985 | 1990 | 1995 | 2000 | 2003 |

1963–1975
Vietnam War

1940s to early 1990s
Cold War

2003
The War in Iraq begins.

KEY IDEA

After World War II, the suburbs grew, roads and transportation expanded, and America, again, became involved in more wars.

WORDS TO UNDERSTAND

beltway
boom
communist
department store
minority
threaten

Veterans Come Home

After World War II, thousands of men and women who had served our country in many parts of the world came home to Maryland. Their families were happy to have them home again.

To thank veterans for their service to our country, the government paid for their college education. This program was called the G.I. Bill of Rights. Getting a college education helped veterans learn the skills they needed to get good jobs. Then, when they finished school, there were plenty of jobs available. Maryland industries had stopped making war supplies and returned to making products for people to buy.

Soldiers were excited to come home after the end of World War II. **How do you think they felt when they arrived in the United States?**

There was a housing boom after World War II. **What clues from this picture tell you that it is a historic image?**

The Building Boom

Many returning soldiers got married and started families. They wanted a nice place to live. People wanted space where their children could play. Companies began building houses and new communities for young families. This sudden need for family housing caused a building *boom*. It also increased the need for building materials, such as wood and bricks.

Many of these new houses were built outside the cities, in the suburbs. Before long, roads and houses were being built where farms used to be. As people began moving to the suburbs, so did many businesses. People could then shop and get good jobs outside of the cities.

New Problems

As families moved away from the cities and bought cars, cities needed fewer trolleys and buses. People who did not have cars had trouble getting to work and to stores. Fewer people meant cities got less tax money. Soon, there wasn't enough money to pay for good schools. Many of the people who stayed in the cities were poor. Crime became a problem, which caused more people to move out of the cities. Once these troubles began, it was hard to turn things around.

In the 1950s, more and more suburbs were built outside of cities, where more land was available. Compare this drawing to the earlier drawing on page 217. **What changes do you notice?**

Life in the Suburbs

Life in the suburbs was different from in the cities. Some communities made rules people in the cities did not have. Some had rules that said people had to keep their grass cut. Some had rules about who could or could not buy a house in the community. Many new suburbs would not sell homes to blacks or Jews. In other parts of the country, Asian people and those who spoke Spanish could not live in certain neighborhoods. While some people loved living in the suburbs, others did not. Many **minorities**, or people who made up a small part of the population, found the suburbs to be very unfriendly and unwelcoming.

Shopping in the suburbs was different from in the cities, too. Instead of walking to the small grocery store on the corner, people drove to large supermarkets. Supermarket owners built large parking lots for all the cars. The Hecht Company opened the first suburban department store in Silver Spring. A **department store** is a very large store that sells many different products. Stores in the cities opened branches in the suburbs. The Harundale Mall, in Glen Burnie, became the first covered shopping mall in the state.

Chapter 10: Modern Maryland

Transportation Expands

Maryland built new roads for all the new cars. The U.S. government spent a lot of money on highways that stretched all across the country. Many people got jobs building these highways. The highways had many lanes and no stoplights. Cars could travel long distances quickly.

Roads and Bridges

Two new roads in Maryland that connected suburbs to city streets were the Baltimore Beltway and the Washington Beltway. A *beltway* is a highway that goes around a city.

The Chesapeake Bay Bridge, near Annapolis, was built to connect the Eastern Shore to the Western Shore. The bridge changed the Eastern Shore in many ways. Land that had been covered with farms was soon covered with stores, motels, and gas stations. Ocean City became a crowded resort. In time, weekend traffic jams became more and more common.

The government paid for highways to be built across Maryland and throughout our country. **Why do you think the pattern these highways makes is called a cloverleaf?**

Air Travel

Before World War II, very few people traveled by airplane. Today, we fly across the country and around the world for business, vacation, and to visit friends and family. The Friendship Airport opened. Today, we call it the Baltimore-Washington Thurgood Marshall International Airport, or BWI. It was named in honor of Marylander Thurgood Marshall, the first African American justice to serve on the U.S. Supreme Court. A justice is a judge.

More people started to travel by airplane at this time. **Do the insides of airplanes look similar today to how they looked in the past?**

Modern Inventions

Cars and airplanes were not the only new inventions that changed people's lives. Many inventions we take for granted today were first used after World War II. Most families started buying televisions. At first, TV programs were all in black and white and only on for a few hours each day. Shows like *I Love Lucy* were very popular. Have you ever seen re-runs of the old black-and-white TV shows?

"I was in first grade when my family got our first television set. . . . I was the second person in my class to have a TV. One morning a week there were two shows for children. My whole class would walk to my house or to my friend's house to see the shows. Our mothers gave everyone a lollipop or cookies."

—Sue Ellery

Many families got their first TV in the 1950s. **How are TVs different today than they were in the past?**

What Do You Think ?

After televisions came air conditioners, computers, DVD players, and cell phones. In what ways have these things changed our lives?

Korean War

Korea had been divided into two parts at the end of World War II. North Korea had a **communist** government, which was run by a dictator. This government owned most of the property. It could tell people where to live and work.

South Korea had an elected government. It was an ally of the United States. North Korea invaded South Korea. North Korea wanted to unite all of Korea under the communist government.

Many nations sent troops to help South Korea fight communism. The United States was one of those nations. Soldiers from Maryland fought in Korea. After three years, both sides agreed to stop fighting. Korea was still divided, but American soldiers finally returned home. Some of your grandfathers or great-grandfathers may have been soldiers in Korea.

Many Koreans had to leave their homes because of the war. **What do you think life was like for these people?**

The Korean War Veteran's Memorial is in Washington, D.C. **What do you think the statues represent?**

THE COLD WAR

The United States and the Soviet Union took part in the Cold War. Both countries competed with each other to be the strongest. The Soviet Union was communist and supported communist countries. The United States was free and supported non-communist countries.

Several times the Cold War became "hot" when there was fighting, as in Korea. Most of the time, the two large countries threatened each other. To *threaten* means to warn that something bad might happen. They also gave money and weapons to smaller countries where there was military fighting.

The United States and Soviet Union

The United States and Soviet Union were involved in the Cold War for many years. **Which country was the largest?**

Soviet soldiers were always on guard and ready to fight. **What do you think the mood in America and in the Soviet Union was like during the Cold War?**

New Weapons

The United States and Soviet Union also tried to build and store the most weapons. Both countries developed new bombs that were more powerful than the atomic bombs used against Japan. People were very afraid because of all the new weapons.

The government opened public bomb shelters. People built shelters in their backyards. Schools across the country practiced what to do if a bomb were dropped. They taught students to duck under their desks or to move quickly to the basement. Students sat against a wall while their teacher read to them until the drill was over.

Many families built bomb shelters to protect themselves in case the Soviets attacked our country. **How would you have felt if you had to stay in this shelter for several days or weeks?**

① KEY IDEA REVIEW

1. How were cities affected when many people moved to the suburbs?
2. What transportation changes happened after World War II?
3. In communist countries, who owned most of the property?

KEY IDEA

The civil rights movement, the women's movement, and the Vietnam War challenged Maryland and our whole country.

WORDS TO UNDERSTAND

civil rights
ideal
illegal
race
violent
wage

Hard Times for African Americans

In Maryland, as in many states, schools were segregated. Black kids went to one school, while white kids went to another. Most schools for blacks did not have new buildings, books, science labs, or gyms like the schools for whites had. Schools weren't the only places where blacks and whites were segregated.

African Americans faced other challenges. They were not allowed to have certain jobs. Most hotels, restaurants, theaters, and even parks did not admit black families. Some theaters made African Americans sit in the balcony.

People who were protesting segregation at the Gwynn Oak Amusement Park in Baltimore County were arrested. The protestors sang songs as they waited to be arrested. **What do you think the people's mood was as they protested?**

Doctors in Maryland have helped develop *vaccines*, or shots, for diseases like polio, measles, and rubella. A team at Johns Hopkins discovered a way to help babies born with a serious heart problem. They figured out a way to open up a baby's chest and operate on the heart. Their work has prevented the death of thousands of babies.

The Shock Trauma Center is located at the University of Maryland Hospital. *Trauma* is a serious injury. The hospital treats people who have suffered serious injuries. Dr. R. Adams Cowley discovered that patients treated soon after their injuries recovered better than those who had to wait for treatment. He called this important time the "golden hour." He helped thousands of people survive after getting seriously hurt.

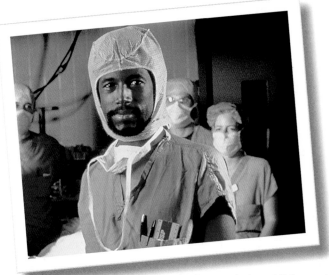

Dr. Benjamin Carson helps children who have had serious brain or spine injuries. **What do you think a day at work is like for Dr. Carson?**

Helicopters quickly carry patients to the Shock Trauma Center at the University of Maryland Hospital. **Have you ever seen a medical helicopter flying overhead?**

Lesson 3: Modern Marylanders

MARYLANDERS IN SPACE

Maryland has played an important role in the exploration of outer space. A lot of the research to learn more about the universe that our planet Earth is a part of has taken place in our state.

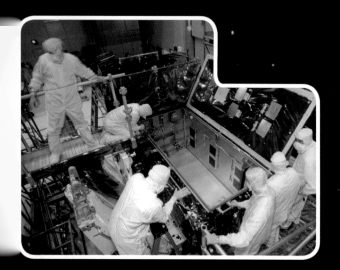

The Goddard Space Flight Center in Greenbelt is part of the National Aeronautics and Space Administration, or NASA. *Aeronautics* is the science of flight. Here, scientists are learning about the Earth and the universe. One of the ways they do this is by using satellites and other tools that help them observe what goes on in space.

Astronauts at the Goddard Space Flight Center prepare supplies to go onboard space shuttles. **Why do you think these astronauts are wearing clean, white clothing while they are working?**

Another important tool scientists use to study space is the telescope. Have you ever looked through one? Did you see the stars and planets? Scientists at the Space Telescope Science Institute in Maryland developed a very powerful telescope. It is called the Hubble Space Telescope. This very large telescope was created to circle, or *orbit*, the Earth. Its job is to send thousands of pictures from space back to scientists. This way we can see some of the things that happen in space.

The Hubble Space Telescope takes pictures as it orbits the Earth. **What do you think the astronaut in this picture is doing?**

MARYLAND'S ASTRONAUTS

Robert Curbeam studied at the U.S. Naval Academy in Annapolis. He became an astronaut. Curbeam's first mission in space lasted 12 days. During his career, Curbeam participated in three space flights and walked in space seven times. After 13 years as an astronaut, he retired from NASA. Curbeam enjoys biking, weight lifting, and spending time with his family.

Robert Curbeam

Marsha Ivins has participated in five space flights. One of her jobs while in space was to help put satellites in position. She has traveled to the International Space Station and docked at the Russian space station, Mir. The team's mission at Mir was to move people and supplies between spacecrafts. When Ivins is not working, she likes flying airplanes and baking.

Marsha Ivins

Dr. Thomas Jones has traveled into space on four important missions. He helped set a shuttle record by spending almost 18 days orbiting the Earth. He was also a mission specialist for the space shuttle *Endeavour*. Dr. Jones has spent more than 52 days in space. He has done 3 space walks. In his free time, he enjoys reading, playing baseball, hiking, biking, camping, skiing, and flying.

Dr. Thomas Jones

Modern Immigrants

The world seems to be getting smaller. Telephones, the Internet, and fast transportation have brought people around the world together. Today, many people move from one country to another. Are any students in your class from different countries?

New Cultures Add Richness

Over the centuries, immigrants have brought their languages, religions, and cultures to America. People have come here from Europe, Africa, Asia, and Latin America. A century ago, some new Marylanders spoke Italian, Greek, Polish, or Yiddish. Today, some Marylanders speak English in school and another language, such as Spanish, Korean, or Ibo, at home.

People from other countries also have brought their religions with them. Some are Christians, and some are Jews. In recent years, Muslims and Buddhists have come to Maryland.

Cultural celebrations and festivals teach us about the customs and traditions of people from different places. You can taste new foods, listen to music from around the world, and sometimes watch special dances.

Sharing Traditions

People take their traditions with them when they move. In America, we enjoy food and music from all over the world. For example, immigrants from the Caribbean brought reggae music. Spaghetti came from Italy and tacos from Latin America. Newcomers usually begin to celebrate American holidays, such as Thanksgiving, even though these holidays might not have been celebrated in the country where they were born. New immigrants learn to enjoy and value the diversity of people in America.

On India Day, everyone is welcome to come and learn about the culture of India. **Can you describe the traditional Indian clothes that these people are wearing?**

Many people from Mexico and Central America have come to live in Maryland. They grew up speaking Spanish. **Can you read the signs in both English and Spanish at this festival in Maryland?**

Chapter 10: Modern Maryland

Spotlighting Geography

Changes Are Both Good and Bad

Often things that affect the land are partly good and partly bad. Think back over all things that affected the land that were described in this chapter. Choose one topic to write a two-paragraph essay about. In the first paragraph, describe how the change was good. In the second paragraph, describe how the change was bad.

Here's an example of an essay. In the first paragraph, you could describe how the changes people have made to the land affect the environment. In the second paragraph, you could discuss your opinion about how much growth is good.

Becoming a Better Reader

Recognize Cause and Effect

You have learned that good readers use several strategies to understand new information. Another of these strategies is recognizing cause and effect. Every event has a cause, or reason, behind it. Every event also has an effect, or consequence. Some events have more than one cause and more than one effect. Choose an event from the chapter, such as the civil rights movement or the Cold War. Describe one cause and one effect of the event in a complete paragraph that includes a topic sentence and three or four supporting sentences.

Reviewing What You Read

1. What was the G.I. Bill of Rights?
2. In your own words, describe the differences between suburbs and the cities.
3. Why was Thurgood Marshall's role in the Supreme Court significant?
4. In what ways do different cultures enrich life in Maryland today?
5. What solutions would you suggest to help put an end to inequality among people?
6. Do you agree that we need plans like Smart Growth to protect our environment? Why or why not?

Our Government

What's the Big Idea?

Our government is run by the people we elect. Its job is to protect the people and their rights.

The Maryland State House, which is our state's capitol, is located in Annapolis. **Can you point to the Maryland State House with the white steeple in the center of this picture?**

11

There are three levels of government—national, state, and local. The national government is the government for our whole country. In addition, each state also has its own government. Counties, cities, and towns also have local governments.

Our government is run by the people we elect. All people, including kids, have rights and responsibilities. It is the government's job to protect our rights. In return, we all must work to make our country, state, and communities good places to live by being good citizens. We can be good citizens by obeying laws and respecting one another. Good citizens are also educated about the issues facing our country. They take part in their communities. One of the most important ways they do this is by voting.

KEY IDEA

Our government is a democracy that is divided into three levels and three branches.

WORDS TO UNDERSTAND

advisor
checks and balances
democracy
enforce
execute
federal system
interpret
jury
legislate
rule of law

The U.S. Capitol Building in Washington, D.C., is where some members of the national government meet. **Can you find the Statue of Freedom on the top of the dome of the building?**

Our Government

Government is very important in the history of our nation and state. Our system of government is called a *democracy*, which means government by the people.

The Purpose of Government

Our government has many jobs. One of its most important jobs is to provide safety and order. The police and military protect us from harm. Laws protect us by setting rules that people must obey. The government *enforces*, or carries out, these laws and punishes people who break the laws.

Another important job of government is to protect our rights. These rights are very important in our democracy.

Sometimes it is hard to balance these two jobs. Too much order could mean that we might lose some of our important rights. However, if people could do whatever they wanted, we would have no order and everyone would suffer. Government officials work to keep a good balance between these two jobs.

History of Our Government

Over 200 years ago, the 13 colonies decided to tell the Britis[h] king that they were breaking free. They would start their own country with new ideas about freedom and government.

The Constitution of the United States

The Founding Fathers wrote our country's Constitution, wh[ich] set up the government that we have today. The Constitution states that the government is responsible to the people. It also guarantees certain rights for all of us. The Constitution is the basis of our government.

A Federal System

The Constitution established a *federal system*. Under this system, we have both a national government (also called the federal government) and state governments. The Constitution gives some powers to the national government and some powers to state governments.

The Founding Fathers did not want a king or queen to govern America. **How can you tell this man is a king?**

The U.S. Constitution is the set of ideas and rules for our government. **What are the first three words of the Constitution and why do you think those words were used?**

285

Branches of Government

The Constitution established a national government. It divided the power among these three branches of government. The men who wrote the Constitution did this so that no one person or small group of people would have all the power. The three branches of our national government are the legislative, executive, and judicial.

Legislative Branch

The legislative branch *legislates*, or makes laws. It is called the U.S. Congress. Congress is made up of two parts called houses: the U.S. Senate and the U.S. House of Representatives. Congress also has the power to tax people and to declare war.

In the Branches of Government Tree, find the people giving speeches about the laws they want passed.

Executive Branch

The executive branch executes the laws of the legislative branch. To *execute* means to put into effect. The president is the head of the executive branch. The president is elected by the whole country. The president suggests new laws, meets with leaders of other countries, and is in charge of the military.

It is the president's job to run the country. He or she chooses many men and women to help do this. The president's top *advisors* are called the cabinet. Cabinet members head the government departments like the Department of Education and the Department of State.

In the Branches of Government Tree, find the reporters asking the president questions. What would you ask the president if you had the chance?

286

Judicial Branch

The judicial branch says what the laws mean. In other words, it *interprets* the laws. It decides whether or not laws that have been passed fit with the U.S. Constitution. The judicial branch is made up of the Supreme Court and the lower courts.

The courts also decide if a person has broken the law. Anyone accused of a crime has a right to a trial by jury. The *jury*, made up of 12 citizens, listens to all the evidence in a trial. Then, the jury decides whether the person accused of the crime is guilty or not guilty.

In the Branches of Government Tree, find the judge and jury.

Balance of Power Protects Our Rights

Having three branches of government means that no one branch has all the power. The legislative branch, the executive branch, and the judicial branch divide the power. The power is balanced among the three branches. Sometimes this balance of power is called *checks and balances*. Our system of checks and balances means that no one branch of government can take power away from the other branches. Each branch checks the power of the other branches. This division of power helps protect our rights.

Rule of Law Protects Our Rights

Another way that our rights are protected is called the *rule of law*. All our laws are written down. We can read the laws and know exactly what the laws are. These laws are the same for everybody. No one, rich or poor, is above the law. No one can make up new laws just because he or she feels like it. The Constitution spells out how laws can be made. Representatives we elect have to approve them.

Police officers help to enforce the laws. **Have you ever seen a police officer riding a bike in your city?**

What Do You Think?

What do you think life would be like with no rules? Do you think a system with no rules would work well?

Levels of Government

The United States of America is the full name of our country. Our country is made up of 50 states that work together. That is why we call ourselves "united."

Our Founding Fathers wanted to be sure that government did not become too powerful. One of the ways they made sure this did not happen was by dividing the government into different levels.

Our government is divided into three levels. The national government is the highest level of government. It makes decisions that affect everyone in the country. The state governments are the second highest level. Each state government makes decisions for the people in that state. Below the state governments are the local governments. Local governments make decisions for people in counties, cities, and towns. You will learn more about state and local governments later in this chapter.

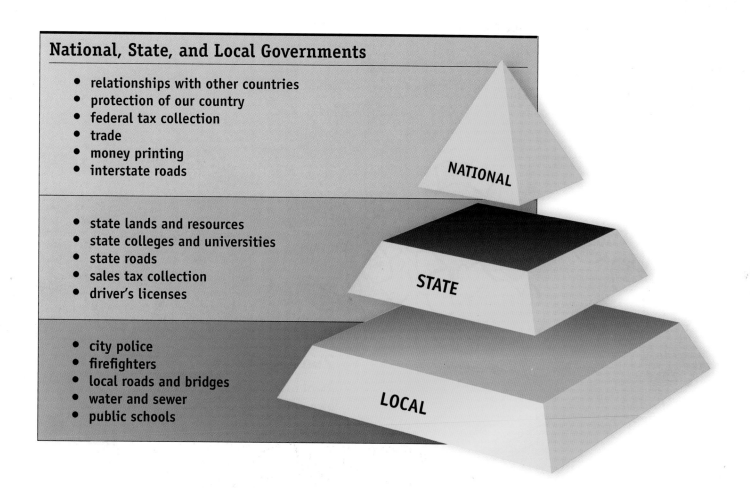

National, State, and Local Governments

- relationships with other countries
- protection of our country
- federal tax collection
- trade
- money printing
- interstate roads

NATIONAL

- state lands and resources
- state colleges and universities
- state roads
- sales tax collection
- driver's licenses

STATE

- city police
- firefighters
- local roads and bridges
- water and sewer
- public schools

LOCAL

The Bill of Rights

Many people liked the new Constitution and the way the government was set up. But others worried that people's rights would not be protected. They asked for a document that would clearly state the rights of every American. Ten amendments, or additions, were added to the Constitution. These amendments are called the Bill of Rights. It is the government's job to make sure these rights are protected.

1ST AMENDMENT

Freedom of religion: People can worship as they wish or not at all. The government cannot choose one religion for the whole country.

Freedom of speech: As long as their words do not cause danger to or harm other people, people can express their opinion about any subject without being arrested. People can even complain about the government.

Freedom of the press: The government cannot tell people what they can and cannot print in newspapers or books.

Freedom of assembly: People can join and meet with any group. However, they cannot commit crimes with the group.

2ND AMENDMENT

Right to bear arms: Adults can own guns for legal activities.

3RD AMENDMENT

Right to not house soldiers during peacetime: Kings used to make people house soldiers in their homes, but the 3rd Amendment ended this requirement.

4TH AMENDMENT

Freedom from improper search and seizure: The police can only search through a person's things if they have good reason to believe the person has something illegal.

5TH, 6TH, AND 7TH AMENDMENTS

The 5th, 6th, and 7th amendments protect people accused of a crime. They include the right to a quick trial and a trial by jury.

8TH AMENDMENT

The government is not allowed to punish people in a cruel way.

9TH AMENDMENT

People can have other rights not named in the Bill of Rights.

10TH AMENDMENT

The national government does not have all the power in the United States. State governments also have power.

1 KEY IDEA REVIEW

1. What is the purpose of our government?
2. What are the first 10 amendments to the Constitution called?
3. What are the three branches of government?
4. What are the three levels of government?

What Do You Think?

Does freedom of speech mean you can write graffiti on public property? Can you tell lies that harm others? How can we use our freedoms so they don't hurt anyone else?

KEY IDEA

Our state government is made up of three branches that make and enforce state laws and help protect our rights.

WORDS TO UNDERSTAND

appeal
dispute
foundation
governor
responsibility
unconstitutional
veto

Maryland's State Government

The 50 states of our country have different geography, people, and industries. This means each state has different problems and needs that state governments take care of.

The Maryland State Constitution

The Maryland State Constitution is the *foundation*, or basis, of our state government. It defines the basic laws for our state. Our state constitution begins with the Declaration of Rights, which is similar to the Bill of Rights in the U.S. Constitution. The declaration guarantees freedom of religion, speech, and assembly. It guarantees that the press will be free to report the news. It guarantees people accused of a crime will have the right to trial by jury. Maryland's Declaration of Rights also declares that all taxes must be voted on by the legislature that is elected by the people.

Members of the Maryland House of Delegates meet in the State House in Annapolis. **Can you point to the people who have come to watch the meeting of the elected officials?**

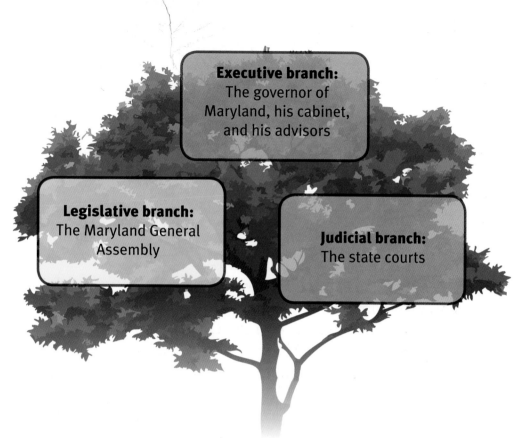

Executive branch: The governor of Maryland, his cabinet, and his advisors

Legislative branch: The Maryland General Assembly

Judicial branch: The state courts

Three Branches of Maryland Government

Like the national government, the state government is divided into three branches. Each branch has *responsibilities*, or duties. That way the power is balanced just as it is in the national government.

Legislative Branch

The Maryland General Assembly is our state's legislative branch. It is made up of two houses—the State Senate and the House of Delegates. These two houses meet in Annapolis, our state capital. Marylanders elect men and women to represent us in the General Assembly.

The General Assembly makes laws for Maryland. It decides on taxes. It approves the budget for our state. A budget is a plan for how money will be spent. In other words, it decides how Maryland will spend the money it collects in taxes. The General Assembly also approves certain officials appointed by the governor.

Some Powers of the Maryland General Assembly
- Makes laws for the state
- Decides on taxes
- Passes the budget for our state
- Approves certain officials

Members of the General Assembly

All citizens of Maryland who are 18 years or older can vote for the members of our General Assembly. We choose men and women whose ideas we like. If they do not pass the laws we want them to, we can choose new representatives at the next election.

Maryland is divided into 47 State Legislative Districts. Each district sends one state senator and three state delegates to Annapolis. Elections for these members of the General Assembly are held every four years.

Executive Branch

The **governor** is the head of Maryland's executive branch of government. He or she has many important jobs.

The governor signs bills that have been passed by the General Assembly into law. Sometimes the governor does not like a bill that the General Assembly has passed. When this happens, he or she can **veto**, or reject, it. When the governor vetoes a bill, it usually does not become a law.

The governor also makes up the budget for the state. He or she gives it to the General Assembly for the members to vote on. They can approve it or not approve it. The governor and the members of the General Assembly discuss the budget until they can agree on how to spend the state's money.

It is the governor's job to run the state. He or she chooses a lot of men and women to help do this. They make up the governor's cabinet.

Many state employees do the day-to-day work of running the executive branch. Some help people get licenses to drive cars or run businesses. Others inspect farms and factories. Some work to protect our health and the environment. Others inspect roads and bridges to make sure they are safe. Some work in our state universities. State workers do a lot of different jobs.

Every four years, the citizens of Maryland vote to elect the governor. This election happens at the same time that we elect members of the General Assembly.

Some Powers of the Governor
- Enforce the laws of Maryland
- Sign bills into law or veto them
- Prepare the state budget
- Appoint judges to state courts
- Maintain law and order in the state

Governor Martin O'Malley

Maryland's Governor Martin O'Malley grew up in Montgomery County. He later moved to Baltimore City. He loved politics and began volunteering to help people who were running for office when he was in college. The first time he ran for election, he did not win. O'Malley also ran for office a second time and did win. He was elected to the Baltimore City Council. He served for eight years. He was elected mayor of Baltimore when he was only 36 years old.

In 2006, he was elected governor of Maryland. Since he has been governor, O'Malley has been working hard on improving our schools, cleaning up the Chesapeake Bay, and taking care of the state's finances.

O'Malley and his wife have four children: Grace, Tara, William, and Jack. They all live in the Governor's Mansion in Annapolis. For fun, O'Malley plays guitar in a rock band called O'Malley's March.

Lieutenant Governor Anthony Brown

Maryland's Lieutenant Governor Anthony Brown was born in New York State. Anthony Brown served in the Maryland House of Delegates before he was elected lieutenant governor. Being lieutenant governor is like being vice president of the United States. If the governor can no longer serve, the lieutenant governor becomes the governor of our state. Anthony Brown also takes on various jobs that the governor asks him to do. He has worked a lot on education and health care issues.

Anthony Brown's parents were immigrants. His father came to the United States from Jamaica and his mother came from Switzerland. They made sure their five children got a good education. After college, Brown joined the Army and was a helicopter pilot. Then, he went to law school and became a lawyer. Brown has two children, Rebecca and Jonathon.

Judicial Branch

Maryland's judicial branch of government is made up of our state courts. The judges in our courts are experts on Maryland's constitution. The courts uphold our constitution. They decide whether or not laws that have been passed fit with the state constitution. If the court decides that a law goes against some part of Maryland's constitution, then that law is *unconstitutional*. This means it cannot be a law any longer. No law can take away people's rights that are listed in the U.S. or state constitution.

Another important job of the courts is to hold trials. One of the rights guaranteed to us in the U.S. Constitution and by the Maryland constitution is trial by jury. If someone is accused of committing a crime, he or she has a right to have a trial. A jury of 12 citizens is chosen to hear the evidence. The evidence consists of all the facts about the case. After listening to the evidence, the jury then decides if the person on trial has been proven guilty of committing a crime.

Settling *disputes*, or arguments, is another thing that the courts do. For example, a person might ask the courts to decide who is to blame for an accident. The court will listen to both sides and then decide who caused the accident. That person will then have to pay to repair the damage.

Some Powers of the Maryland Courts
- Decide if state laws fit with our constitution
- Conduct trials of people accused of crimes
- Settle disputes

The Maryland Court of Appeals

The Court of Appeals is the highest court in Maryland. It is like the Supreme Court of the United States, but it decides cases only in Maryland.

If someone does not like the decision of a lower court, they can *appeal* that decision. The Maryland Court of Appeals reviews the ruling. Once the Court of Appeals makes its decision, it is final.

The Maryland Court of Appeals is the highest court in Maryland. **How many judges serve on the Maryland Court of Appeals?**

Police officers help enforce the laws in our communities. They also often take part in community activities. **Can you describe what is happening in this picture?**

Obeying the Laws

One way you can be a good citizen is to obey the laws. We will all have a cleaner place to live if people obey the law and don't litter. We will have a safer place to live if everyone obeys the traffic laws. What other laws must we all obey?

Respecting Each Other

Respecting the rights of others is an important way to be a good citizen. The U.S. Constitution guarantees all of us rights like freedom of speech and freedom of religion. We can help protect these rights by respecting people who have ideas that are different from ours. They, too, have a right to speak their ideas. We can also respect people whose religion is different from ours. Our Constitution guarantees that each of us has the right to worship as we choose. By respecting other people's choices, we are helping to preserve our democracy.

Educated Citizens

Knowing about our country, state, and communities is an important part of being an educated citizen. We should know what is happening in the world around us. We should all be educated about our government. We should know how it works.

An educated citizen is a powerful citizen. You have learned about our government in this chapter. You are becoming an educated citizen.

Learning About Issues

It is important to know what issues face us today. Every period in history has had challenges. Issues affect everyone, including children. You have read about a lot of issues as you have studied Maryland's history. What are some of the major issues facing us today?

There are lots of ways to get information about what is going on in the world, in our country, in Maryland, and in your own neighborhood and school. Here are some ways you can learn about what is happening:

- Watch the news on television.
- Look up information on the Internet.
- Read newspapers and books.
- Talk with grown-ups, such as your family members and your teacher.

Computers are a great resource to find information about current issues. **Have you ever read the news on the Internet?**

Different Ideas About How to Solve Problems

People don't always think alike. People don't always agree about what the government should do to solve problems in our country and state. In a democracy, different people have different ideas. They have different *perspectives*, or points of view, on how to deal with our problems and how to meet our needs. Let's look at a few of today's problems. We will also consider some of the ideas that people have about policies to solve them. A *policy* is a course of action people decide on to deal with an issue.

Health Care

Do you ever go to the doctor when you are sick? Do you think it is important for everyone to be able to go to a doctor when they are sick? One issue today is that some people don't have enough money to pay to see a doctor.

Some people want the government to make sure that all people have good *health care*, so that everybody can see a doctor when they are sick. Some people do not want to pay tax money to the government to help pay for other people's health care. They believe all people should pay for their own health care. Some people say that health care will not be as good if the government oversees it. What is your perspective on this problem?

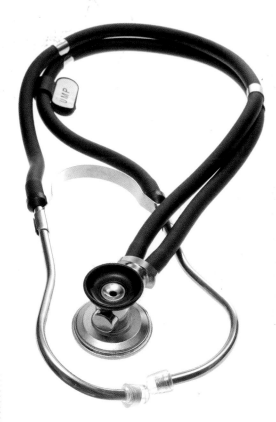

Linking the Present to the Past

Preventing injuries is an important part of modern health care. One hundred years ago, this was not the common practice. In the factories, unsafe machines injured workers. These workers were then fired because they could not do their jobs any more. Today, the government regulates workplace safety. Some people think it is right for the government to protect workers by making safety regulations. Other people say that is none of the government's business and that business owners should make their own rules. Which perspective do you agree with? Why?

Public Schools

Lots of people are worried about public schools. Across Maryland, some schools have very good resources—new books, maps, art supplies, and sports fields. Other schools do not have enough resources because they cannot afford to buy them.

Some people think the state should give more money to the schools in areas that don't have enough resources. Other people say that it is not fair to take money from the people that pay taxes in one county and spend it on the schools in a different county. What do you think?

Linking the Present to the Past

Today, all children are required to go to school until they reach the age of 16. One hundred years ago, many children worked in factories and on farms instead of going to school. They earned money for their families. Some people wanted the government to pass a law requiring children to go to school. Other people felt that parents should decide whether or not their children would go to school.

Some public schools have more supplies than other schools.
What resources are the students in this picture using?

It is necessary for all people to help take care of the Earth. **What are these children doing to help?**

The Environment

People have built homes, roads, and businesses on land that used to be forest or wetlands or that was used for farms. All of this building is one cause of pollution of our land and water.

Some people say that we need to cut back on building. They say we need to protect the land. Other people say that we should build more homes and businesses. They say that this makes jobs and brings more people and more money to our state.

People in different parts of the state often care about different issues. People who live near the Chesapeake Bay are concerned about *pollutants*, or things like chemicals and waste that end up in the bay and make it dirty. People in Western Maryland live near the state's mines. They want the mines to clean up the pollution they make. How do you think Maryland should take care of the environment?

What Do You Care About?

You have seen that there are many issues to think about and care about. You can influence your government to take action on an issue that you care about a lot.

Would you like someone to plant grass and trees in a vacant lot near your home? Would you like to have a playground in your neighborhood? Would you like your school to get new books? Would you like to be sure that everyone has good health care? Would you like to help clean up our water and air?

We may not be able to fix every problem all at once, but there are ways to start making changes.

In 2008, Americans elected a new president of the United States. Barack Obama won by a large majority in Maryland and across our country. Obama promised change at a time when we were troubled by bad economic problems, two wars, and many environmental problems.

Many young people were strong supporters of Obama. They worked hard to try to get him elected. Young people put up signs and made phone calls for their candidate. Many 18-year-olds registered to vote for the first time, and many of them voted for Obama.

Making Your Voice Heard

There are lots of ways children can influence government. Our elected officials know that you will all be voters when you are older, so they will listen to you. You can write letters to the governor or mayor. You can also write letters to state senators or delegates. You can invite your state delegate or your city council person to come visit your class.

Voting

One of the most important things that every citizen can do is vote. Plan to vote as soon as you are old enough. When you vote, you help choose the men and women who make our laws and spend our tax money. If you don't vote, you will lose the opportunity to have a say in how our government is run.

You can also encourage the adults in your family to vote. At election time, ask them which **candidates** they are voting for and why. Ask if you can go with them when they vote.

MARYLAND SOCIAL STUDIES SKILLS AND PROCESSES

SKILLS

Recognize the Importance of Voting

It takes many leaders to run our country, state, and cities. These leaders do important work that affects your life. Citizens of Maryland have a responsibility to take part in electing good leaders. Talk to adults in your school, family, and community about voting. Ask them how they feel about being able to vote. Ask them to explain why voting is a:

- right
- privilege
- responsibility

Write down their answers. Be ready to share them with your class. As a class, talk about what would happen if no one cared about voting. What would happen if only a few people voted?

Make posters urging people to vote. Hang them around town before the next election.

Chapter 12

Economics in Maryland

Economics is the study of how people produce, buy, and sell goods and services. Different countries have different economic systems.

To buy goods and services, people need money. People work to earn money.

It is important to understand how to best prepare yourself to earn a living. It is also very important to learn how to make wise choices about saving and spending the money you earn.

Maryland has a fast-growing economy. Medicine, technology, fishing, farming, mining, and tourism are some of the largest industries in our state.

What Is Economics?

The study of how people produce, sell, and buy goods and services is called *economics*. People need food, clothing, and shelter. We want books, games, and bicycles. All these items are called goods or products.

Sometimes people need medical care from a nurse or doctor. Sometimes people need to have their leaky roof or broken window fixed. People who help us or do things for us provide *services*.

Economic Systems

An economic system is a way of producing and selling goods and services. Different countries use different systems, but all economic systems answer three basic questions:

- What goods should be produced and what services should be provided?
- How will goods be produced and services provided?
- Who will buy goods and services?

In the United States, people, not the government, own most of the companies. Company owners decide what products to produce and sell or what services to provide. They also decide where their company will be located, how much the company will charge for their products or services, and who will work for them.

When we are sick, we sometimes go to a doctor. **Does a doctor provide a good or service when she examines a child who has a sore throat?**

Entrepreneurs work hard to earn a profit by selling their goods or services. **What does this man, who owns a stand along Route 33 between Easton and St. Michaels, sell?**

Businesses Produce Goods and Provide Services

Businesses exist to meet people's needs. They produce goods and services that people want to buy. New businesses open to provide new, better, or less expensive products or services.

Businesses Take Risks

People who own their own business are called **entrepreneurs**. Entrepreneurs hope to make a profit by selling their goods or services. **Profit** is the money left over after a company has paid all of its expenses. Business owners have many different kinds of expenses. They pay for the materials to make their products. They pay **employees**, or workers, to make products or provide services. They also pay rent for their factory, store, or office building.

Entrepreneurs take risks. Their business might not succeed. Many times they start their business with their own money. Sometimes they take out bank loans they have to repay. What happens if no one wants their product or service? What other risks might entrepreneurs face?

Lesson 1: Basic Economics

Businesses Make Choices

Business owners make a lot of choices. Companies choose what they will make or what services they will provide. Each company has only so many resources and so much money. A company that makes candy has to buy the ingredients and the machines it needs to manufacture the candy. It has to pay its workers. The company probably does not have the resources to buy materials to make toys as well. By choosing to make candy, the company gives up the opportunity to make toys. This is called *opportunity cost*.

Businesses Specialize

Many businesses *specialize*. This means they provide products or services related to one thing. For example, some businesses provide medical care, some build homes, and some sell food.

Within these businesses, there is further specialization. Within the medical field, there are hospital workers, nurses, doctors, and dentists. Home builders also specialize. Some build the frame for the house. Others build the roof. Some install the plumbing.

Specialization allows people to learn a lot about their job. They are experts at what they do. This means consumers can expect high-quality goods and services.

Because most workers have a specialty, we all have to depend on each other. A plumber might not know how to repair a car. A teacher probably doesn't have time to grow all of his or her own food.

Some construction companies specialize in building homes. **What specialized work are the men in this picture doing?**

Businesses Set Prices

How do business owners decide how much to charge for their products? The selling price depends on a lot of things. For coats, it might depend on how much the cloth and zippers cost.

The price may also depend on how many coats are for sale. If a coat becomes popular, the company might not be able to make enough for all the people who want one. If many people want the same coat, they may be willing to pay more.

Sometimes a store has too many coats. If people don't want to buy the coats, the store may need to lower the price so more people will buy them.

Competition

A company may want to lower its prices so it can sell more products. What if two or more companies make the same thing? What happens if one of them charges less for its products? More people would probably buy the product that costs less.

Price is one way companies compete, but there are many other ways. Companies may choose to make new products. They may work to make better ones. They may offer better services. That is *competition*.

Companies sometimes decide to sell their products at a lower price for many reasons. **Why do you think the Hoop Magic store decided to have a sale?**

Scarcity

Scarcity also affects the price of products and services. *Scarcity* occurs when there is not enough of something that people want.

Think of the gasoline that your parents use to fill up the car. Gas is made from oil. A lot of the oil we use in the United States comes from other countries. Sometimes there are problems with buying oil from these countries. When there are problems, sometimes gasoline is scarce and the price goes up.

Scarcity can also be caused by lack of natural resources. If we use up our resources, companies will not be able to produce what we want to buy. For example, people are concerned we may run out of oil in the future. When that happens, how will we run our cars, trucks, buses, airplanes, and other vehicles?

Scarcity is when there is not enough of a product that people want to buy. **Is the demand for gas at this gas station high or low?**

Advertising

Companies spend a lot of money on advertising to sell their product or service. Many companies advertise on the radio, TV, and Internet. They also run ads in newspapers, in magazines, and on billboards.

Businesses use different types of advertisements. Some ads claim you will look better, you will be healthier, or people will like you more if you buy their product or service. Sometimes they say that movie stars use their products. Companies often say their product is new and improved.

Wise consumers understand how advertising works. Have you ever bought something because an ad made it seem exciting and then you found out it wasn't? Do you always believe everything an ad claims?

Coca-Cola used this ad to sell their product. **Why do you think the company put Santa Claus in the ad?**

Government's Role in the Economy

The government plays an important role in our economy. The government **regulates**, or makes rules for, businesses and workers. The government enforces these rules so that the products and services businesses provide are safe.

The government is also an employer. The government employs people to provide goods and services for communities. The government also buys many goods and services for our country, state, and local communities. For example, the government gives schools money to buy books, paper, and pencils, and fire departments money to buy fire trucks.

In addition to regulating businesses, the government also prints paper money and mints, or makes, coins. Each state has its own quarter. **What is pictured on this quarter?**

Government Sets Rules for Businesses

The government regulates products companies produce. For example, companies are not allowed to use paint with lead on children's toys. This is because lead is poisonous, especially to children. The government also inspects food to make sure it is safe for people to eat.

The government makes rules workers must follow. For example, the government requires truck drivers to have special licenses to drive big trucks. The government requires that all doctors complete a certain amount of schooling and pass certain tests. Would you want to be treated by just anybody who claimed he or she was a doctor?

The government also sets the minimum wage. This is the lowest wage that companies are allowed to pay workers. We want all people who work to earn enough money to buy the things their families need.

Food Labels

The government makes rules about the food we buy. One rule requires food companies to make a list of what is in their products. That way people will know what they are eating. They will know if a certain food has a lot of sugar or fat. They will know if it has vitamins. This requirement is an example of government regulation. Have you seen labels like this on your food?

Nutrition Facts

Serving Size 1 Cake (43g)
Servings Per Container 5

Amount Per Serving

Calories 200 Calories from Fat 90

	% Daily Value*
Total Fat 10g	15%
Saturated Fat 5g	25%
Trans Fat 0g	
Cholesterol 0mg	0%
Sodium 100mg	4%
Total Carbohydrate 26g	9%
Dietary Fiber 0g	0%
Sugars 19g	
Protein 1g	

Vitamin A 0%	•	Vitamin C 0%
Calcium 0%	•	Iron 2%

* Percent Daily Values are based on a 2,000 calorie diet. Your daily values may be higher or lower depending on your calorie needs:

		Calories:	2,000	2,500
Total Fat	Less than		65g	80g

The government regulates how much of certain resources businesses can use. **What natural resource is this truck hauling?**

Government Regulates Resources

In some cases, the government regulates how businesses can use resources. The government plays an important part in regulating the use of resources so there will be plenty available for our children and our children's children. The government also makes regulations for companies. For example, the government regulates how companies mine and burn coal in order to lessen water and air pollution. The government also owns a lot of land. It regulates how much timber companies can cut from the land.

Government Uses Tax Money

All businesses pay taxes. When a business makes a big profit, it pays a lot of money in taxes. If a business does not make much money, it does not pay as much in taxes. The government uses tax money to pay for schools, health care, road repairs, and other goods and services. All citizens benefit from this.

Grown-ups have to fill out a tax form that lists how much money they earned during the previous year. **What is the title of this tax form?**

Form 1040
Label
(See instructions on page 16.)
Use the IRS label. Otherwise, please print or type.
Presidential Election Camp...
Filin...
Department of the Treasury—Internal Revenue Service
U.S. Individual Income Tax Ret
For the year Jan. 1-Dec. 31, 2006, or other tax year b
Your first name and initial
If a joint return, spouse's first
Home address (
City

Government Buys Goods and Services

National, state, and local governments buy goods and services. National government pays for military supplies. State governments pay for supplies for state colleges. Local governments pay for supplies for police and fire stations. The government makes jobs for the people who produce the goods and services it buys.

However, even the government has limited resources and has to make choices. If the government orders 100 airplanes for the Air Force, this decision creates a lot of work for companies that manufacture airplanes. On the other hand, if the government decides not to order any new airplanes for the military, some companies will lose profits and some workers may lose their jobs.

If the government buys 100 airplanes, it may not have the money to help build new schools. If the government pays for new schools, it may not have as much money for health care services. As you learned, this is called opportunity cost.

The government pays for Apache helicopters to be built for the military. **Inside what kind of building do you think this picture was taken?**

1 KEY IDEA REVIEW

1. What is economics?
2. What is an opportunity cost and how does it affect how people spend their money?
3. Give an example of how our government regulates business.

In 2006, on average, people without a high school diploma earned $20,510 a year and people with a college degree earned $46,440 a year.

Office workers, doctors, and teachers all provide valuable services. **What job would you like to do when you grow up?**

How People Make, Save, and Spend Money

People do various jobs to earn money. People save some of the money they make to pay for things in the future. The choices people make affect how much money they earn.

People Make Money

People want to make a good income so they can buy the things they want. A *salary* is the money a person earns for doing a job. How can you make sure you will earn a good salary? The choices you make will affect how much money you will earn.

Your education affects how much money people make. People who finish high school usually make more than those who don't. People who finish college usually earn more than those who don't.

People's skills and interests can also affect what job they choose. Some people have special skills. A person who enjoys writing might become a reporter. Maybe you like working with children and will become a teacher.

Career choices affect how much money people make. A *career* is a job that a person usually goes to school or receives special training in order to do. A person often stays in the same career for his or her whole life. A nurse makes more than a teacher even though both jobs require about the same amount of education. People who specialize in their career also normally make more money. A heart surgeon makes more money than a family doctor.

People save money so they can buy things in the future. **Do you have a piggy bank like this one?**

Your Paycheck and Taxes

Once you begin working, you will receive a paycheck from your employer. Let's say you earn $10 an hour, and you work 40 hours per week. You will not receive the full $400 in your paycheck. There will be **deductions**, or money taken out of your paycheck, usually in the form of taxes.

Every worker pays taxes to help pay the bills of our communities, state, and country.

Local governments collect taxes to pay for fire departments, police departments, schools, and libraries.

The state of Maryland collects taxes to pay for roads, universities, health care, and prisons.

The federal government collects taxes to pay for highways, national parks, and the military.

What would happen to your community without these government services?

People Save Money

Money is important to people. Without it, people could not buy the things they need. People often come up with plans to buy things they want in the future. Suppose you get an allowance from your parents. Maybe you earn money for walking the dog or taking out the trash. Let's say you earn $10 each week, and you want to buy a scooter that costs $100. How long will it take to get the scooter if you save $10 each week?

Most people save their money in a bank. But why should they put money in a bank? Why not just save the money in a shoebox under the bed?

Banks provide a service for storing money. They provide savings accounts. When you put your money in the savings account, the bank can use your money until you want it back. The money the bank pays you to keep your money in a savings account is called *interest*. Would money in a shoebox under your bed earn interest?

People Spend Money

People are workers. They are also consumers. A *consumer* is a person who buys goods and services. Anyone who spends money is a consumer. Are you a consumer? What kinds of things do you buy with your money?

Whenever you buy something, you are making a choice. Sometimes you have to choose not to buy one thing so you will have enough money to buy something else. As you know, this is called opportunity cost.

Credit Cards

People often use credit cards, instead of cash, to pay for goods and services. When people buy something with a credit card, they get the good or service now, but they pay for it later. Credit card companies charge people interest to use the card if they don't pay the bill off right away. By the time the consumer has paid the bill plus interest, he or she has paid more for the good or service than it cost.

Credit cards allow people to buy goods and services now and pay for them later. **When did this credit card expire?**

What Do You Think❓

How do you feel about credit cards? Is it a good idea to buy things now and pay for them later? Why or why not?

People Create a Budget

Adults think a lot about how to spend their money. They often make a budget. A *budget* lists the money a person expects to get and how he or she will spend the money. A budget helps people manage their money and make wise spending choices.

Most people want to spend their money wisely. They want to get the most they can for their money. They compare prices of products at different stores. They also compare the prices of different brands of products.

Different Economic Groups

Most families have enough money to pay for their expenses, but they do not have enough to buy everything they want. We call this economic group the middle class.

A few Americans are very wealthy or part of the upper class. They own more than one home. Some own a private airplane or several vacation homes. They do not have to worry about paying medical bills, college tuition, or for other large expenses.

About 10% of all American families live in poverty. They may not have enough money to pay the rent or even buy enough food. They may not be able to pay a doctor when they are sick. Often, they have not finished high school, so they do not have the skills to get good jobs. Sometimes medical bills or another large expense has taken all their money. Many Americans believe that we live in such a wealthy country that no one should ever be homeless, hungry, or without medical care.

SKILLS
MARYLAND SOCIAL STUDIES SKILLS AND PROCESSES

Study a Budget

Creating a budget is one good way to practice your math skills. Study this sample budget.

Monthly Income = $3,000

Expenses	
House payment	$1,200
Electricity/water	$100
Car	$350
Gasoline	$100
Food	$500
Clothes	$150
Savings	$100

1. How much is the house payment?
2. Add up all of the expenses. What is the total?
3. How much money is left over after all the expenses are subtracted from the monthly income?
4. Can you think of other expenses that should be included in this budget?
5. Is there enough left over to buy a $300 TV?

Sharing Money

In an earlier chapter, you read about philanthropists who lived 100 years ago. Do you remember what a philanthropist does? A philanthropist shares his or her money to help other people.

There are many philanthropists in Maryland today who have given money to organizations that make communities nicer places to live. Businessman Eddie Brown and his wife, Sylvia, have given money to a Maryland college and library and to a scholarship program for Baltimore middle school children. Businessman Joseph Meyerhoff and other members of his family have given money to the Baltimore Symphony Orchestra. His son, Harvey, has given money to a Maryland hospital and a museum in Washington, D.C. Baseball player Eddie Murray has given money to a nature center. Baseball player Cal Ripken has given money to educational programs.

MARYLAND PORTRAIT

Eddie Brown
b. 1940

Eddie Brown grew up on a farm in Florida with his grandparents. There was no hot water or indoor plumbing. Brown helped his grandfather pick oranges and grapefruits. When Brown was 13, his grandmother died and he went to live with his mother in Pennsylvania. He was the first person in his family to graduate from high school. He then graduated from college.

After completing his education, Brown got a job helping people make money in the stock market. After working for the Maryland company T. Rowe Price, Brown decided to start his own business called Brown Capital Management. It was very successful, and he and his wife became wealthy.

The Browns share their wealth with others. They have given away millions of dollars.

2 KEY IDEA REVIEW

1. Explain how education affects income.
2. How does a budget help a person make choices about spending?
3. Why do some people give money to organizations?

Our Economy in the Past

Maryland's economy has changed over the years. It is much different now from the way it was a few hundred years ago. Some of the industries that were very important in the past are not as important today. There are also many new kinds of industries today that did not exist in the past.

As soon as colonists arrived here, they planted food. They had to grow or hunt everything they ate. There were no grocery stores. The settlers used local materials, mainly wood, to build their homes. They cut down trees because they could not buy wood. They did all the work themselves.

In the early days, the colonists imported things like hammers, nails, sewing needles, and fabrics from England. Products that came all the way from England were very expensive.

As more people settled here, they brought their skills with them. Marylanders began making furniture, clothing, boots, and other goods people needed. They made bricks for building. They made tools. Because Maryland was on the water, people used ships for transportation and trade. Soon, Maryland had busy shipyards, and many people made their living building and repairing ships.

KEY IDEA

A strong economy is an important part of what makes Maryland a good place to live.

WORDS TO UNDERSTAND

disability
high-tech
non-profit
organic
software
tourism

Some of the industries that were important in Maryland in the past have changed. **How is the way clothes are made different today from in the past?**

Agriculture

Agriculture has always been important in Maryland. In early Maryland, most people were farmers. A lot of farmers grew tobacco. At the time of the American Revolution, Maryland grew a lot of grain. The grain was shipped to soldiers. Maryland became known as the "Breadbasket of the Revolution." After the war, farmers hauled grain, vegetables, and fruits on wagons to nearby cities and towns to sell.

Once railroads were built, people shipped farm products more easily across the country. After people started to can foods, farm products could be preserved for a long time and shipped even farther. Marylanders canned fruits, vegetables, and even oysters.

The Industrial Revolution

During the Industrial Revolution, factories were built in Maryland. In the late 1800s and early 1900s, Maryland had a lot of factories. Large mills used coal and iron to make steel for railroad cars and tracks.

The Industrial Revolution meant a lot more goods could be produced and sold. Clothing was mass-produced in Maryland factories. Clothing prices went down. As prices went down, people could afford to buy more clothes. Instead of just buying one pair of pants, a person might be able to buy three pairs of pants.

Factories opened in Maryland cities during the Industrial Revolution. This factory produced ammunition. **What clues in this drawing tell you that this is not a modern factory?**

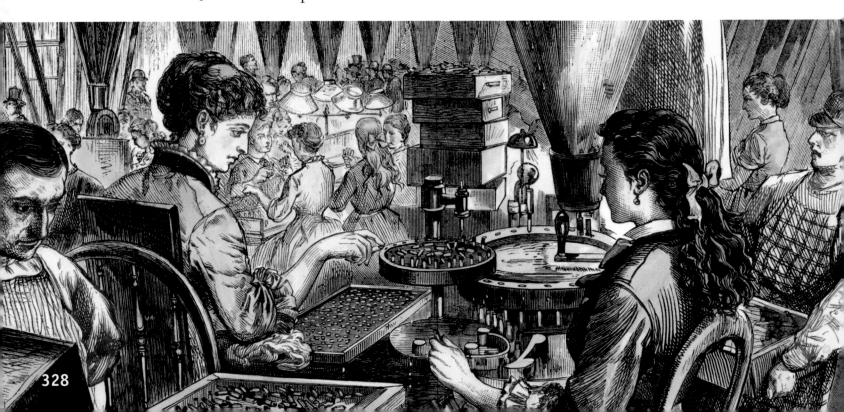

Our Economy Today

Modern Marylanders do many different kinds of work. Our state produces a variety of goods and services. Marylanders today work at jobs in the fields of science and medicine, technology, fishing, farming, tourism, and mining and for non-profit organizations. As you read about the work people in our state do, think about which industries the people you know work in.

Seafood from the Chesapeake Bay is sold in Maryland and shipped to other states and countries. **What does this sign advertise?**

Fishing is a large industry in Maryland. **Have you ever seen a fishing boat like this one returning to harbor?**

BP Solar uses technology to capture energy from the sun. **Can you describe the high-tech workplace where this woman does her job?**

Technology

New high-tech industries are very important in our state's economy. *High-tech* industries use new technologies to make products. Maryland companies develop parts and programs for computers. People do research to try to improve technology. Some work to come up with better ways for people to communicate by phone and computer. People are also developing products for use in outer space. Other people are working to help us understand the human body better and to improve health.

Many high-tech industries are located in Maryland. A lot of our state's technology companies are located in the area around Baltimore and Washington, D.C., and in Howard, Anne Arundel, and Frederick Counties. The headquarters of BP Solar USA is in Frederick. It makes solar panels that use the sun to make clean energy for homes and businesses. A company called SafeNet in Belcamp makes *software*, or programs used by computers, to protect the information stored on computers. Proteus Technologies, with bases in Annapolis Junction and Columbia, develops computer software and designs computers.

New Technology

Life has changed a lot over the last century. One big reason is technology. Inventors have come up with a lot of new ideas, and companies have made a lot of new products.

In the early 1900s, the invention of the telephone allowed people across the country to talk to one another. Automobiles gave people the freedom to travel wherever they wanted to go. Radios allowed people to get the latest news and listen to the same programs. Later, TV did the same thing.

Refrigerators made it possible to store many foods. Before families had refrigerators, they had iceboxes. An iceman, who usually arrived in horse-drawn wagon, delivered a big chunk of ice. This ice block sat in the bottom of the icebox to help keep food cool. Electric refrigerators kept food much colder, so it lasted longer.

Airplanes made it possible for people to fly long distances. People could travel across the United States or across the ocean in just a day on an airplane. A train trip across the United States in the 1920s took four or five days. A ship's journey across the Atlantic Ocean took even longer. Mail also could be sent on airplanes, speeding up its delivery to far-away places.

Technology is changing how we live very quickly. Computers and the Internet have brought a world of information right into our homes and schools. You can find out almost anything by going online. You can also communicate instantly with people all over the world. You can e-mail a friend, read newspapers from around the world, and do research on any topic. Over a period of just a few years, the Internet has totally changed the way we connect with the world.

Many people today no longer have home phones. Instead, they depend on their cell phones. Cell phones allow us to be in constant contact with other people wherever we are. We also have other new technologies today. For example, many people have MP3 players that allow them to download and store thousands of songs.

Technology companies work hard to produce products people will buy. Most technology products are developed over many years before they are sold in stores. It takes a lot of work and money to develop these products. Think about how much people spend on these products today. Products our grandparents never even dreamed of are things we consider necessary today. Technology has made a huge difference in the way people live.

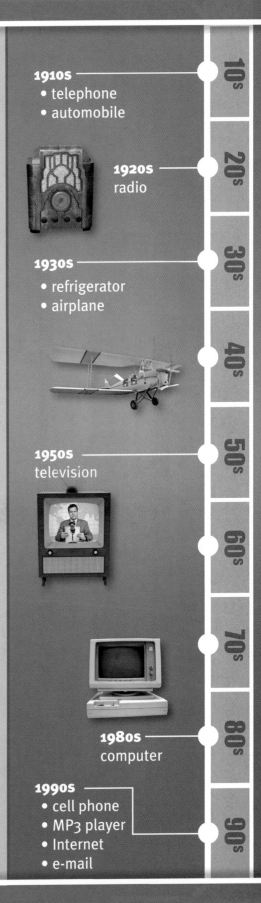

1910s
- telephone
- automobile

1920s
radio

1930s
- refrigerator
- airplane

1950s
television

1980s
computer

1990s
- cell phone
- MP3 player
- Internet
- e-mail

10s 20s 30s 40s 50s 60s 70s 80s 90s

Fishing

All of the waterways around Maryland produce seafood. The waters of the Atlantic Coastal Plain are especially good for fishing. Watermen live and work near the Chesapeake Bay and the rivers that flow into the bay.

Crabs, clams, oysters, and fish are shipped to all parts of the United States and to countries around the world.

Farming

Farming is important in many regions in our state. The Atlantic Coastal Plain is flat with fertile soil, so a lot of farming is done there, especially on the Eastern Shore. Corn, soybeans, tomatoes, and melons are major products of the Atlantic Coastal Plain. Many farms raise chickens and other animals. Big companies like Perdue have built plants to process chickens in our state.

The Piedmont and Appalachian regions are also good for farming. Maryland farmers in the hilly Piedmont area grow a lot of wheat. They also grow fruits like apples and many kinds of vegetables. Dairy farms produce milk and cream. Farmers in the Appalachian region even grow Christmas trees.

Some Marylanders are *organic* farmers. They grow crops naturally. They do not use chemicals to kill insects or weeds.

Our state grows a lot of its own food. We also ship some of our farm products to other states and around the world.

Family Tradition and the Economy

Tradition is important in many Maryland businesses. Tradition is the handing down of ways of doing things from one generation to the next. Many farmers are the sons and daughters of farmers. Many watermen grew up helping their fathers who were also watermen. Do you have any relatives who have followed in the footsteps of their parents or grandparents?

Farming is important in Calvert County. **In what season was this picture taken?**

Tourism

When people visit Maryland, they can see history come alive in St. Mary's City, go crabbing on the Chesapeake Bay, go canoeing on one of Maryland's rivers, hike in our state's mountains, or cheer at a Baltimore Orioles game. People can visit the Maryland Zoo, National Aquarium, Maryland Science Center, and many museums. During the summer, thousands of people visit Ocean City for a vacation. This is all part of *tourism*—a major industry in Maryland.

People who visit Maryland spend money on transportation, hotels, food, entertainment, and recreation. All of these things make money for the businesses and workers of Maryland.

Mining

Coal miners work in the Appalachian region in Western Maryland. Cumberland became a major manufacturing center, in part because of the nearby coal. Coal was used for fuel in the factories. One big problem with coal is that when it is burned, it causes air pollution. Today, scientists are working to find ways to burn coal without causing so much pollution.

Many tourists visit the Ocean City boardwalk, where there are many shops and restaurants. **What sweet treat is available from a store shown in this picture?**

Regional Jobs

People do special jobs in some regions of our state. Different jobs are available in different areas because of differences in geography and natural resources. Some people who live near the Chesapeake Bay have jobs in the seafood industry. Farming is important in areas of our state where the soil is good. Mining is important in Western Maryland.

Regional jobs depend on the natural resources available in particular regions of Maryland. **What natural resources might this mining company depend on?**

MARYLAND PORTRAIT

Dr. Alfred Sommer
b. 1942

Dr. Alfred Sommer is a doctor and teacher at Johns Hopkins. He was concerned that many children around the world, especially in poor countries, were going blind. He wanted to help these children. He also wanted to prevent other children from losing their sight.

First, he had to do research to find out the cause of the problem. Dr. Sommer guessed a lack of vitamin A caused the problem. He thought adding more vitamin A to the children's diets might prevent blindness. He tested his ideas and discovered he was right. Because of Dr. Sommer's work, many children around the world can still see.

Science and Medicine

Maryland is a center of scientific and medical research. Both the Johns Hopkins University and the University of Maryland have medical schools, where students study to become doctors. The Johns Hopkins Hospital in Baltimore is known around the world for medical research and treatment.

Maryland companies and organizations also develop and manufacture medicines. Novavax, in Rockville, develops new vaccines. Scientists do medical research at the new East Baltimore Biotech Park. The National Library of Medicine in Bethesda is the largest medical library in the world.

Government Jobs

Many people in Maryland work for the federal government. Marylanders commute to government jobs in Washington, D.C. They also work at federal government jobs in Maryland at places like the Goddard Space Center in Prince George's County and the Social Security headquarters in Baltimore County. Social Security is a federal government program. Other people work for the military at bases like Fort Meade, Aberdeen Proving Ground, and Andrews Air Force Base.

Any airplane that is carrying the president of the United States is called Air Force One. Air Force One is based at Andrews Air Force Base in Prince George's County, Maryland. **What words are painted on this plane?**

Marylanders also work for our state government and local governments. Some people work at state government jobs in Annapolis and other Maryland cities. Other people work for local governments. If you attend a public school, all of the teachers at your school work for the local government.

The Special Olympics Maryland Baltimore County gives disabled athletes the opportunity to compete in different sports. **Can you describe what is happening in this picture?**

Non-Profit Organizations

One important part of Maryland's economy is our non-profit organizations. ***Non-profit*** means not run for the purpose of making money. They work hard to improve our communities. They pay their employees, but they don't make a profit.

There are many non-profit organizations in our state. Special Olympics Maryland gives athletes with disabilities opportunities to compete. A ***disability*** is a physical or mental challenge. The Maryland Zoo takes care of over 1,500 animals. The Chesapeake Bay Association works to make the bay cleaner and healthier. The NAACP (National Association for the Advancement of Colored People) works to ensure all people have equal opportunities. Many colleges, universities, and hospitals are non-profit organizations. Many religious groups run non-profit organizations to help people who need housing and food.

MARYLAND ENTREPRENEURS

Many people in Maryland are entrepreneurs. They work hard to run successful businesses that serve the needs of their customers well. Sometimes the whole family helps with the business. Let's meet some of Maryland's entrepreneurs.

THE STELZER FAMILY

The Stelzer family owns a toy store called Shananigans. Mother, father, son, and daughter work together selling wonderful toys for boys and girls. They have to know which toys are right for children of different ages so they can help their customers make good choices. The Stelzers do everything to keep their business running smoothly. In addition to selling toys, they take out the trash, dust the shelves, pay the bills, and make phone calls. It takes a lot of hard work to run your own business.

POLLY BART

Polly Bart started a business called Greenbuilders. She designs, fixes up, and builds houses. What she likes best is making the buildings "green." That means she uses materials that are good for our environment. Sometimes she uses recycled materials. Sometimes she puts in sources of "green" power like solar panels. She uses bales of hay in the walls. She designs green roofs, with plants on top of them.

Bart always enjoyed building things. Even when she was young, she liked to use tools. When she was eight years old, she built an underground house. It had two rooms, a dirt chair to sit on, and a plywood roof. Now she makes her living doing what she loves.

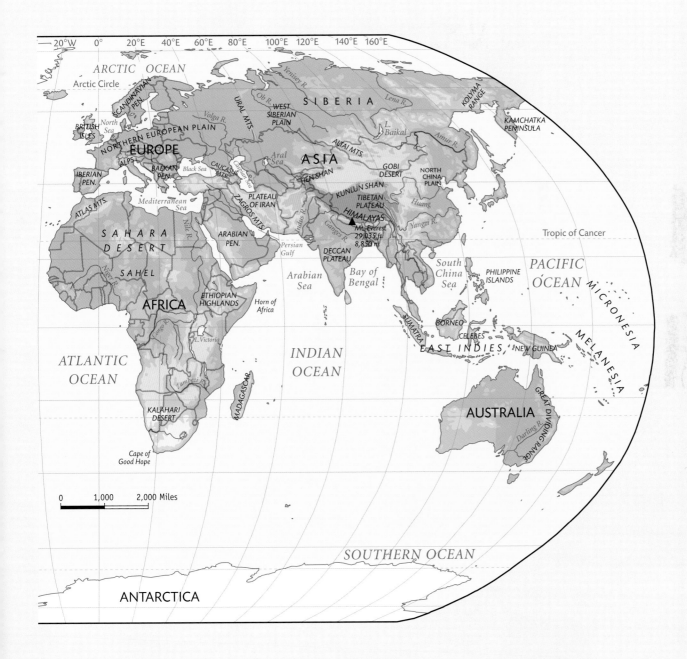

ARCTIC OCEAN
Arctic Circle
SCANDINAVIAN PEN.
BRITISH ISLES
North Sea
NORTHERN EUROPEAN PLAIN
EUROPE
ALPS
IBERIAN PEN.
BALKAN PEN.
Black Sea
CAUCASUS MTS.
ATLAS MTS.
Mediterranean Sea
Volga R.
URAL MTS.
Ob R.
WEST SIBERIAN PLAIN
SIBERIA
Yenisey R.
Lena R.
KOLYMA RANGE
KAMCHATKA PENINSULA
Amur R.
L. Baikal
ALTAI MTS.
ASIA
Aral Sea
Caspian Sea
TIEN SHAN
GOBI DESERT
NORTH CHINA PLAIN
ZAGROS MTS.
PLATEAU OF IRAN
KUNLUN SHAN
TIBETAN PLATEAU
HIMALAYAS
Huang
SAHARA DESERT
Nile R.
ARABIAN PEN.
Persian Gulf
Indus R.
Ganges R.
Mt. Everest 29,035 ft. 8,850 m
Yangzi R.
Tropic of Cancer
SAHEL
Niger R.
Arabian Sea
DECCAN PLATEAU
Bay of Bengal
South China Sea
PHILIPPINE ISLANDS
PACIFIC OCEAN
MICRONESIA
AFRICA
ETHIOPIAN HIGHLANDS
Horn of Africa
Congo R.
L. Victoria
SUMATRA
BORNEO
CELEBES
EAST INDIES
NEW GUINEA
MELANESIA
ATLANTIC OCEAN
INDIAN OCEAN
MADAGASCAR
Zambezi R.
KALAHARI DESERT
AUSTRALIA
GREAT DIVIDING RANGE
Darling R.
Cape of Good Hope

0   1,000   2,000 Miles

SOUTHERN OCEAN

ANTARCTICA

20°W 0° 20°E 40°E 60°E 80°E 100°E 120°E 140°E 160°E

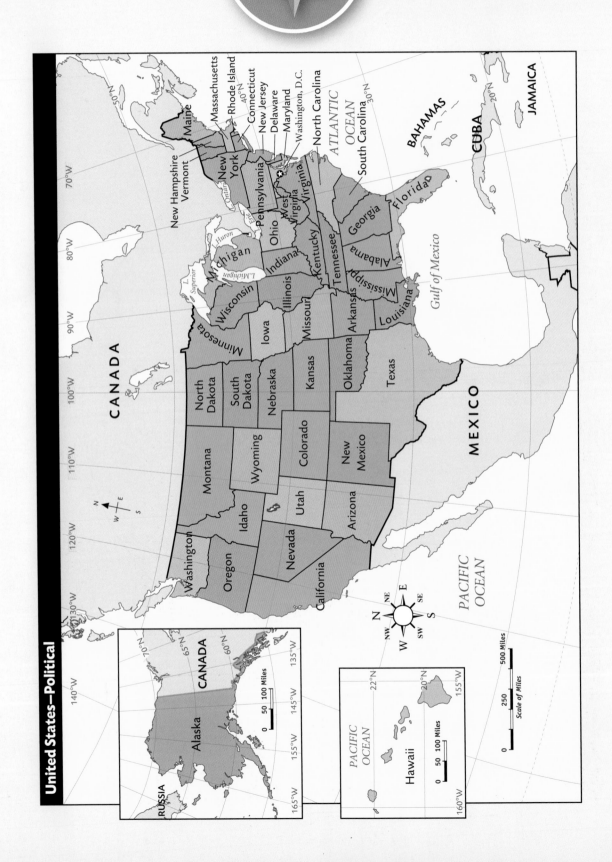

United States—Political

ATLAS

344

ATLAS

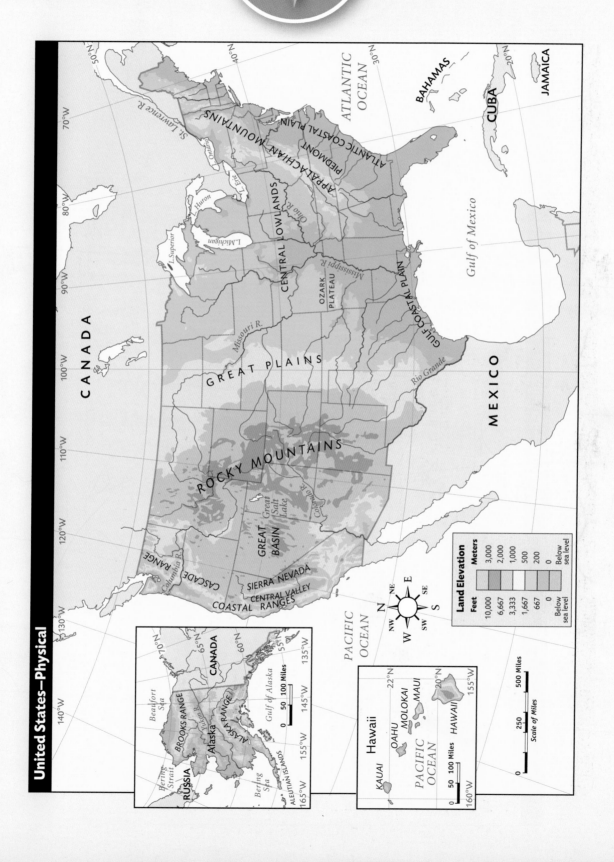

United States—Physical

Land Elevation

Feet	Meters
10,000	3,000
6,667	2,000
3,333	1,000
1,667	500
667	200
0	0
Below sea level	Below sea level

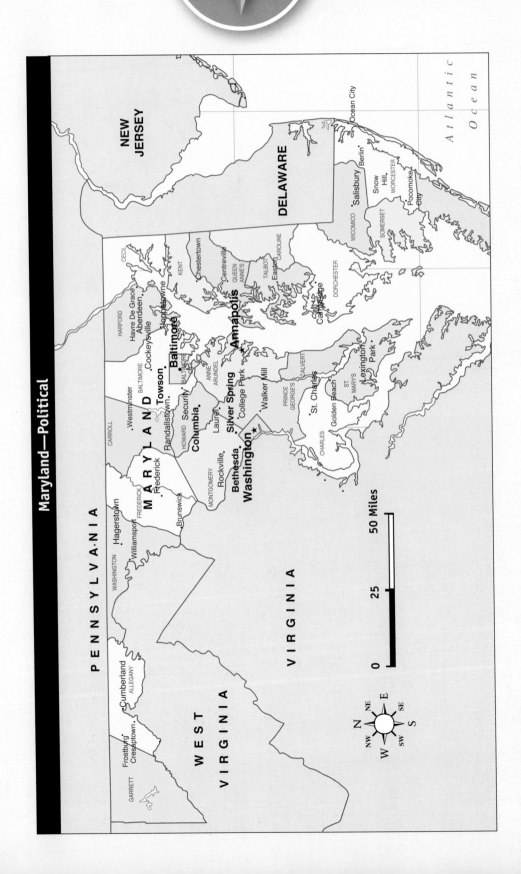

Maryland—Political

PENNSYLVANIA

NEW JERSEY

DELAWARE

Atlantic Ocean

WEST VIRGINIA

VIRGINIA

MARYLAND

GARRETT

ALLEGANY

Frostburg
Cresaptown

Cumberland

WASHINGTON

Williamsport
Hagerstown

FREDERICK

Brunswick

Frederick

CARROLL

Westminster

MONTGOMERY

Rockville

Bethesda

Washington

HOWARD

Columbia

Randallstown

Security

Laurel

Silver Spring

College Park

Walker Mill

BALTIMORE

Towson
Cockeysville

Baltimore

Pikesville

ANNE ARUNDEL

Annapolis

PRINCE GEORGE'S

St. Charles

CHARLES

Golden Beach

CALVERT

ST. MARY'S

Lexington Park

HARFORD

Havre De Grace
Aberdeen

Joppatowne

CECIL

KENT

Chestertown

QUEEN ANNE'S

Centreville

TALBOT

Easton

CAROLINE

DORCHESTER

Cambridge

WICOMICO

Salisbury

SOMERSET

Snow Hill

WORCESTER

Berlin

Ocean City

Pocomoke City

50 Miles

0   25   50

N NE
NW   E
W   SE
SW   S

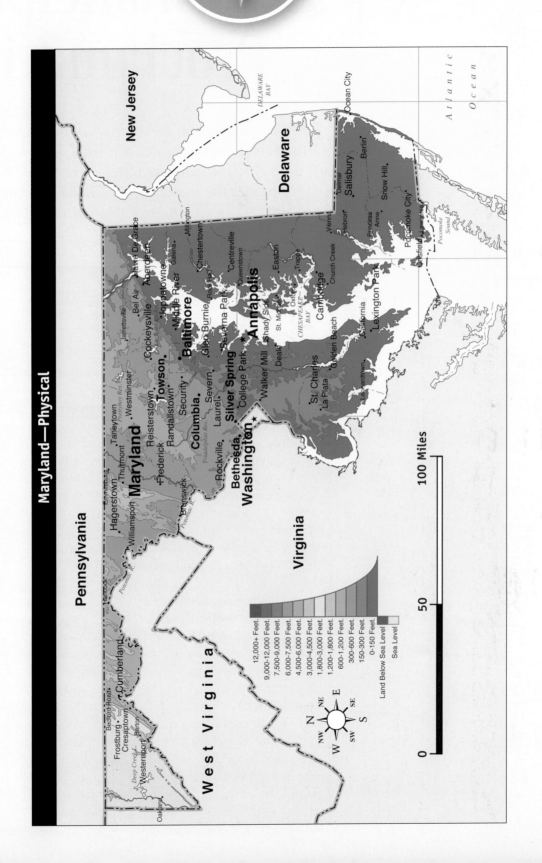

Maryland—Physical

The Emancipation Proclamation

The Emancipation Proclamation was issued by President Abraham Lincoln during the Civil War. It declared that the slaves in the Confederate states were free. This document later became the foundation of the 13th Amendment to the U.S. Constitution.

JANUARY 1, 1863
BY THE PRESIDENT OF THE UNITED STATES OF AMERICA:
A PROCLAMATION.

Whereas, on the twenty second day of September, in the year of our Lord one thousand eight hundred and sixty two, a proclamation was issued by the President of the United States, containing, among other things, the following, to wit: "That on the first day of January, in the year of our Lord one thousand eight hundred and sixty three, all persons held as slaves within any State or designated part of a State, the people whereof shall then be in rebellion against the United States, shall be then, thenceforward, and forever free; and the Executive Government of the United States, including the military and naval authority thereof, will recognize and maintain the freedom of such persons, and will do no act or acts to repress such persons, or any of them, in any efforts they may make for their actual freedom.

"That the Executive will, on the first day of January aforesaid, by proclamation, designate the States and parts of States, if any, in which the people thereof, respectively, shall then be in rebellion against the United States; and the fact that any State, or the people thereof, shall on that day be, in good faith, represented in the Congress of the United States by members chosen thereto at elections wherein a majority of the qualified voters of such State shall have participated, shall, in the absence of strong countervailing testimony, be deemed conclusive evidence that such State, and the people thereof, are not then in rebellion against the United States."

Now, therefore I, Abraham Lincoln, President of the United States, by virtue of the power in me vested as Commander in Chief, of the Army and Navy of the United States in time of actual armed rebellion against the authority and government of the United States, and as a fit and necessary war measure for suppressing said rebellion, do, on this first day of January, in the year of our Lord one thousand eight hundred and sixty three, and in accordance with my purpose so to do publicly proclaimed for the full period of one hundred days, from the day first above mentioned, order and designate as the States and parts of States wherein the people thereof respectively, are this day in rebellion against the United States, the following, to wit:

Arkansas, Texas, Louisiana, (except the Parishes of St. Bernard, Plaquemines, Jefferson, St. John, St. Charles, St. James Ascension, Assumption, Terrebonne, Lafourche, St. Mary, St. Martin, and Orleans, including the City of New Orleans) Mississippi, Alabama, Florida, Georgia, South Carolina, North Carolina, and Virginia, (except the forty eight counties designated as West Virginia, and also the counties of Berkley, Accomac, Northampton, Elizabeth City, York, Princess Ann, and Norfolk, including the cities of Norfolk and Portsmouth[)], and which excepted parts, are for the present, left precisely as if this proclamation were not issued.

And by virtue of the power, and for the purpose aforesaid, I do order and declare that all persons held as slaves within said designated States, and parts of States, are, and henceforward shall be free; and that the Executive government of the United States, including the military and naval authorities thereof, will recognize and maintain the freedom of said persons.

And I hereby enjoin upon the people so declared to be free to abstain from all violence, unless in necessary self defence; and I recommend to them that, in all cases when allowed, they labor faithfully for reasonable wages.

And I further declare and make known, that such persons of suitable condition, will be received into the armed service of the United States to garrison forts, positions, stations, and other places, and to man vessels of all sorts in said service.

And upon this act, sincerely believed to be an act of justice, warranted by the Constitution, upon military necessity, I invoke the considerate judgment of mankind, and the gracious favor of Almighty God.

In witness whereof, I have hereunto set my hand and caused the seal of the United States to be affixed.

Done at the City of Washington, this first day of January, in the year of our Lord one thousand eight hundred and sixty three, and of the Independence of the United States of America the eightyseventh.

By the President: ABRAHAM LINCOLN
WILLIAM H. SEWARD, Secretary of State.

Presidents of the United States

	George Washington **Term:** 1789–1797 **Party:** Federalist[1] **Vice President:** John Adams	**State of Birth:** Virginia **Birth Date:** February 22, 1732 **Death Date:** December 14, 1799
	John Adams **Term:** 1797–1801 **Party:** Federalist **Vice President:** Thomas Jefferson	**State of Birth:** Massachusetts **Birth Date:** October, 30, 1735 **Death Date:** July 4, 1826
	Thomas Jefferson **Term:** 1801–1809 **Party:** Demo-Republican **Vice President:** Aaron Burr, George Clinton	**State of Birth:** Virginia **Birth Date:** April 13, 1743 **Death Date:** July 4, 1826
	James Madison **Term:** 1809–1817 **Party:** Demo-Republican **Vice President:** George Clinton, Elbridge Gerry	**State of Birth:** Virginia **Birth Date:** March 16, 1751 **Death Date:** June 28, 1836
	James Monroe **Term:** 1817–1825 **Party:** Demo-Republican **Vice President:** Daniel D. Tompkins	**State of Birth:** Virginia **Birth Date:** April 28, 1758 **Death Date:** July 4, 1831
	John Quincy Adams **Term:** 1825–1829 **Party:** Demo-Republican **Vice President:** John C. Calhoun	**State of Birth:** Massachusetts **Birth Date:** July 11, 1767 **Death Date:** February 23, 1848
	Andrew Jackson **Term:** 1829–1837 **Party:** Democratic **Vice President:** John C. Calhoun	**State of Birth:** South Carolina **Birth Date:** March 15, 1767 **Death Date:** June 8, 1845
	Martin Van Buren **Term:** 1837–1841 **Party:** Democratic **Vice President:** Richard M. Johnson	**State of Birth:** New York **Birth Date:** December 5, 1782 **Death Date:** July 24, 1862
	William Henry Harrison **Term:** 1841* **Party:** Whig **Vice President:** John Tyler	**State of Birth:** Virginia **Birth Date:** February 9, 1773 **Death Date:** April 4, 1841
	John Tyler **Term:** 1841–1845 **Party:** Whig **Vice President:** None	**State of Birth:** Virginia **Birth Date:** March 29, 1790 **Death Date:** January 18, 1862
	James K. Polk **Term:** 1845–1849 **Party:** Democratic **Vice President:** George M. Dallas	**State of Birth:** North Carolina **Birth Date:** November 2, 1795 **Death Date:** June 15, 1849
	Zachary Taylor **Term:** 1849–1850* **Party:** Whig **Vice President:** Millard Fillmore	**State of Birth:** Virginia **Birth Date:** November 24, 1784 **Death Date:** July 9, 1850
	Millard Fillmore **Term:** 1850–1853 **Party:** Whig **Vice President:** None	**State of Birth:** New York **Birth Date:** January 7, 1800 **Death Date:** March 8, 1874
	Franklin Pierce **Term:** 1853–1857 **Party:** Democratic **Vice President:** William King	**State of Birth:** New Hampshire **Birth Date:** November 23, 1804 **Death Date:** October 8, 1869
	James Buchanan **Term:** 1857–1861 **Party:** Democratic **Vice President:** John C. Breckinridge	**State of Birth:** Pennsylvania **Birth Date:** April 23, 1791 **Death Date:** June 1, 1868
	Abraham Lincoln **Term:** 1861–1865** **Party:** Republican[2] **Vice President:** Hannibal Hamlin, Andrew Johnson	**State of Birth:** Kentucky **Birth Date:** February 12, 1809 **Death Date:** April 15, 1865
	Andrew Johnson **Term:** 1865–1869 **Party:** Union[2] **Vice President:** None	**State of Birth:** North Carolina **Birth Date:** December 29, 1808 **Death Date:** July 31, 1875
	Ulysses S. Grant **Term:** 1869–1877 **Party:** Republican **Vice President:** Schuyler Colfax	**State of Birth:** Ohio **Birth Date:** April 27, 1822 **Death Date:** July 23, 1885
	Rutherford B. Hayes **Term:** 1877–1881 **Party:** Republican **Vice President:** William Wheeler	**State of Birth:** Ohio **Birth Date:** October 4, 1822 **Death Date:** January 17, 1893
	James A. Garfield **Term:** 1881** **Party:** Republican **Vice President:** Chester A. Arthur	**State of Birth:** Ohio **Birth Date:** November 19, 1831 **Death Date:** September 19, 1881
	Chester A. Arthur **Term:** 1881–1885 **Party:** Republican **Vice President:** None	**State of Birth:** Vermont **Birth Date:** October 5, 1829 **Death Date:** November 18, 1886
	Grover Cleveland **Term:** 1885–1889[3] **Party:** Democratic **Vice President:** Thomas Hendricks	**State of Birth:** New Jersey **Birth Date:** March 18, 1837 **Death Date:** June 24, 1908
	Benjamin Harrison **Term:** 1889–1893 **Party:** Republican **Vice President:** Levi P. Morton	**State of Birth:** Ohio **Birth Date:** August 20, 1833 **Death Date:** June 24, 1908
	Grover Cleveland **Term:** 1893–1897[3] **Party:** Democratic **Vice President:** Adlai E. Stevenson	**State of Birth:** New Jersey **Birth Date:** March 18, 1837 **Death Date:** June 24, 1908

William McKinley **Term:** 1897–1901** **Party:** Republican **Vice President:** Garret Hobart, Theodore Roosevelt	**State of Birth:** Ohio **Birth Date:** January 29, 1843 **Death Date:** September 14, 1901
Theodore Roosevelt **Term:** 1901–1909 **Party:** Republican **Vice President:** Charles Fairbanks	**State of Birth:** New York **Birth Date:** October 27, 1858 **Death Date:** January 6, 1919
William Howard Taft **Term:** 1909–1913 **Party:** Republican **Vice President:** James S. Sherman	**State of Birth:** Ohio **Birth Date:** September 15, 1857 **Death Date:** March 8, 1930
Woodrow Wilson **Term:** 1913–1921 **Party:** Democratic **Vice President:** Thomas R. Marshall	**State of Birth:** Virginia **Birth Date:** December 28, 1856 **Death Date:** February 3, 1924
Warren G. Harding **Term:** 1921–1923* **Party:** Republican **Vice President:** Calvin Coolidge	**State of Birth:** Ohio **Birth Date:** November 2, 1865 **Death Date:** August 2, 1923
Calvin Coolidge **Term:** 1923–1929 **Party:** Republican **Vice President:** Charles G. Dawes	**State of Birth:** Ohio **Birth Date:** November 2, 1865 **Death Date:** January 5, 1933
Herbert Hoover **Term:** 1929–1933 **Party:** Republican **Vice President:** Charles Curtis	**State of Birth:** Iowa **Birth Date:** August 10, 1874 **Death Date:** October 20, 1964
Franklin D. Roosevelt **Term:** 1933–1945* **Party:** Democratic **Vice President:** John Nance Garner, Henry A. Wallace, Harry S Truman	**State of Birth:** New York **Birth Date:** January 30, 1882 **Death Date:** April 12, 1945
Harry S. Truman **Term:** 1945–1953 **Party:** Democratic **Vice President:** Alben W. Barkley	**State of Birth:** Missouri **Birth Date:** May 5, 1894 **Death Date:** December 26, 1977
Dwight Eisenhower **Term:** 1953–1961 **Party:** Republican **Vice President:** Richard M. Nixon	**State of Birth:** Texas **Birth Date:** October 14, 1890 **Death Date:** March 28, 1969
John F. Kennedy **Term:** 1961–1963** **Party:** Democratic **Vice President:** Lyndon B. Johnson	**State of Birth:** Massachusetts **Birth Date:** May 29, 1917 **Death Date:** November 22, 1963
Lyndon B. Johnson **Term:** 1963–1969 **Party:** Democratic **Vice President:** Hubert H. Humphrey	**State of Birth:** Texas **Birth Date:** Aug. 27, 1908 **Death Date:** January 22, 1973
Richard M. Nixon **Term:** 1969–1974[4] **Party:** Republican **Vice President:** Spiro T. Agnew, Gerald R. Ford	**State of Birth:** California **Birth Date:** January 9, 1913 **Death Date:** April 22, 1994
Gerald R. Ford **Term:** 1974–1977[5] **Party:** Republican **Vice President:** Nelson R. Rockefeller	**State of Birth:** Nebraska **Birth Date:** July 14, 1913 **Death Date:** Dec. 26, 2006
Jimmy Carter **Term:** 1977–1981 **Party:** Democratic **Vice President:** Walter F. Mondale	**State of Birth:** Georgia **Birth Date:** October 1, 1924
Ronald Reagan **Term:** 1981–1989 **Party:** Republican **Vice President:** George H. W. Bush	**State of Birth:** Illinois **Birth Date:** February 6, 1911 **Death Date:** June 5, 2004
George H. W. Bush **Term:** 1989–1993 **Party:** Republican **Vice President:** J. Danforth Quayle	**State of Birth:** Massachusetts **Birth Date:** June 12, 1924
William J. Clinton **Term:** 1993–2001 **Party:** Democratic **Vice President:** Albert Gore Jr.	**State of Birth:** Arkansas **Birth Date:** August 19, 1946
George W. Bush **Term:** 2001–2008 **Party:** Republican **Vice President:** Richard Cheney	**State of Birth:** Connecticut **Birth Date:** July 6, 1946
Barack H. Obama **Term:** 2009– **Party:** Democrat **Vice President:** Joseph R. Biden	**State of Birth:** Hawaii **Birth Date:** August 4, 1961

* Died in office

** Assassinated in office

1. There were no parties in the first election. The parties formed during Washington's first term.

2. The Republican National Convention of 1864 adopted the name Union Party and renominated Lincoln for president. The Union Party nominated Johnson, a Democrat, for vice president. Although frequently listed as a Republican vice president and president, Johnson returned to the Democratic Party when the Union Party broke apart after 1868.

3. Second nonconsecutive term.

4. Resigned August 9, 1974.

5. Appointed vice president in 1973 after Spiro Agnew's resignation; assumed presidency after Nixon's resignation.

Glossary

A

abolitionist: a person who worked to end slavery

advisor: a person who gives advice to another person

aeronautics: the science of flight

agency: a division of government that manages projects in a certain area

agriculture: the business of growing crops and raising animals to sell for food

alliance: a formal agreement between two countries to support one another

ally: a country or group that helps another country or group protect itself

amendment: a change or addition to the constitution of a state or country

ammunition: bullets, bombs, cannon balls, and other materials that are fired from weapons

ancestor: a past relative

anthem: a song of praise

anti-slavery: opposed to slavery

appeal: to request that a ruling of a court be reconsidered

armed: having weapons

artifact: an object that people who lived in the past made or used and then left behind

assassinate: to murder a person by secret attack often for political reasons

atlatl: a tool that helped early people throw a spear

atomic bomb: a bomb that causes a great explosion due to a sudden release of energy

auction: a sale at which items are sold to people who are willing to pay the most

B

barter: to trade one thing for another without using money

beltway: a highway that goes around a city

biofuel: a fuel made from plants

boom: a sharp increase

boycott: to refuse to buy from a business in order to make a point

budget: a plan for how to spend money

C

campaign: the efforts of a person to try to get enough support to be elected to a political office

candidate: a person who runs for a political office

capital: a city that serves as the seat of government

caption: a description of a picture, drawing, map, or graph

cardinal directions: the four directions (north, south, east, west) on a compass rose

career: a job for which a person usually goes to school or receives special training and to which one usually dedicates his or her life

century: 100 years

ceremony: a formal celebration

charter: a written contract

checks and balances: a system of government in which each of the branches has only certain powers so no one branch becomes more powerful than the others

civil rights: the rights given by the U.S. Constitution and Bill of Rights that belong to every American citizen

civil war: a war between people of the same country

climate: the weather of an area year after year

colony: a settlement or land ruled by another country

communist: based on the principles of communism, a system of government in which the government, not the people, owns all of the land and businesses

commuter: a person who travels back and forth from home to work

competition: the act of competing to be the best or the strongest or to win

concentration camp: a camp where people are held against their will

congregation: a religious group

conquer: to defeat by use of force

consent: to agree

conserve: to protect and save

constitution: a plan for government and the laws it will have

consumer: a person who buys goods and services

contract: a written agreement

convert: to convince a person to accept a religion

council: a group of people that discusses issues

county: a division of land in a state with its own local government

county seat: the town or city where county government offices are located

culture: the beliefs, practices, and way of life of a group of people

custom: a way of doing something

D

debt: money owed

decade: 10 years

declare: to announce

deduction: something that is subtracted or taken away

defend: to protect

degree: a unit of measure for distance around a globe

delegate: a person elected to represent and act for another

democracy: a system of government by the people

department store: a large store with many sections for different products

depression: a period when there are few jobs and people do not have enough money

dictator: a leader who has all the power over a country and its people

disability: a physical or mental challenge

discrimination: the unfair treatment of people

disease: a sickness

disguise: to change the appearance of something

dispute: an argument or disagreement

diverse: having many different characteristics

document: a written paper

drought: a period when there is very little rain

E

economics: the study of how people produce, sell, and buy goods and services

ecosystem: a community of living things

elevation: how high the land is above sea level

emission: something that is given off

employee: a worker; a person who works for a company to earn money

employment: a job

enforce: to carry out

enslave: to make a person a slave

entrepreneur: a person who has an idea for a business and the courage to start the business

equality: the state of being equal

equator: an invisible latitude line that divides the Earth into the Northern and Southern hemispheres

evidence: proof

execute: to put into effect

extinct: no longer living

F

fall line: an imaginary line made by connecting the last waterfalls of rivers

federal system: a system in which there is a national government and state governments

fertile: allowing plants and crops to grow well

flee: to run away from danger

foundation: the basis

freeman: a person who is free; not a slave

frontier: unsettled land

G

generator: a machine that makes electricity

gentry: people who were part of the wealthy class

geography: the study of the Earth's land, water, people, plants, and animals

geothermal energy: heat from inside the Earth

ghetto: a small, crowded area within a city

girdle: to cut away the bark and the layer beneath the bark in order to kill a tree

glacier: a large, slow-moving sheet of ice

glossary: a list of key words found in a book along with their definitions

govern: to rule over

governor: the elected leader of a state

gristmill: a mill for grinding grain

guarantee: to promise

H

health care: having to do with helping people stay healthy and with the treatment of sick people

hemisphere: one-half of the Earth

high-tech: having to do with new technologies used to make products, such as computers

historian: a person who studies history

humid: moist

hunter-gatherer: a person who hunted animals and gathered wild foods to survive

hurricane: a very strong tropical storm

I

ideal: the highest principle

illegal: against the law

immigrant: a person who moves from one country to another country to live

immune: having a resistance to disease

import: to bring goods into a country from another country

income tax: a tax on money people and businesses earn

indenture: a contract that required a person to work for a certain number of years

independence: the state of being independent or not under the control of others

index: a list of topics, which include people, subjects, events, and places, and the page numbers on which information about each of the topics can be found

individual: of, or relating to, one person

industry: a group of similar businesses

inherit: to receive from a family member

interest: the fee charged for borrowing money; the fee paid to a person for money he or she saves in a bank

intermediate directions: the four directions between the cardinal directions on a compass rose (northwest, southwest, northeast, southeast)

interpret: to explain the meaning of something

invade: to enter forcefully, usually with the intent to take over

itinerary: a plan for travel

J

jury: a group of people who listen to a court case and decide if a person committed a crime

K

kerosene: an oil

L

labor union: an organized group of workers who try to get better working conditions and more pay

laborer: a worker

latitude lines: imaginary lines that circle the Earth east and west

lay off: to stop employing

legend: a tool that explains what the symbols used on a map mean

legislate: to make laws

longitude lines: imaginary lines that circle the Earth north and south

lookout: a person who keeps watch over something

luxury: something that people want that is expensive or hard to get

M

manufacturing: the making or producing of goods

mass production: to produce a large number of goods by using machines

mayor: the elected leader of a city

meridian: another name for a longitude line

middle class: the group of people in a society who are not rich or poor

migrant: a person who moves from place to place to find work

migration: moving from one place to another

militia: an army made up of citizens with some military training

minister: a person who leads church services

minority: less than half of the people; a small part of a population

missionary: a person who tries to convert other people to a religion

monarchy: a government ruled by a king or queen

municipal: having to do with a city or town

N

natural resource: something found in nature that people use

neutral: not choosing a side

non-profit: not run with the purpose of making money

O

occupy: to hold control of a land area

opportunity cost: in economics, the giving up of one opportunity in order to pursue another opportunity

orbit: to circle around something

organic: related to the growing of food without the use of chemicals

overland: by, on, or across land

overseer: a person who oversees something

P

paleo: ancient

palisade: a high fence used for protection

patrol: to maintain order and control over an area by carefully passing through it

perspective: point of view; the ideas a person has about something; opinion

philanthropist: a person who donates his or her time or money to a good cause

plantation: a large farm

point of view: a way of thinking about something; opinion

policy: a chosen course of action or way of dealing with something

politics: activities related to running the government and making laws

pollutant: something that pollutes or makes the air, land, or water dirty

pollution: harmful or unclean things in the environment

population: the number of people living in an area

portrait: a picture of a person

poverty: the state of being poor

precipitation: water that falls to the Earth as rain or snow

predator: an animal that lives by hunting and eating other animals

prehistoric: having to do with the time before history was written down

prejudice: a negative judgment made about another person, often based on the person's race or religion

primary source: a firsthand account or original object

privateer: a private ship that is given permission by a country to attack ships from enemy countries

process: to go through a series of steps to prepare something

profit: the money left over after expenses are paid

prohibit: to forbid

proprietor: a person who has control over or owns something

prosperous: having success

protest: to speak out against something

public school: a school that is paid for by the government

Q

quantity: an amount

R

race: a group of people with common ancestors; often refers to skin color

ration: to control the amount of goods that people are allowed to buy

raw material: a material used to make something else

rebel: to fight against people in power

rebellion: an armed fight against people in power

recruit: to convince someone to do certain work

refrigerate: to keep something cold

region: an area of land that shares some common features

regulate: to control according to established rules

religious: having to do with a religion or set of beliefs

renewable: able to be renewed or replaced

repeal: to take away

representative: a person elected to speak, vote, or act for other people

research: careful study to gain understanding

resolve: to find an answer or solution

responsibility: something a person should do; a duty

revolution: a war to replace one government with another government

riot: an angry uprising

route: a chosen course of travel

rule of law: a principle that says that laws apply to all citizens

S

sacrifice: giving up something for the sake of someone or something else

salary: money a person earns for a job he or she does, usually paid out at certain times

sales tax: tax people pay on goods and services they buy

sanitation: the process by which something is cleaned

scale of miles: a map tool that shows distance

scarcity: lack of something

secede: to withdraw; to leave

secondary source: a secondhand account told by someone who heard about, read about, or studied an event or object

segregate: to separate by race

service: work done for another person for money

settlement: a place or region that people have recently settled

software: programs used by a computer

solar panel: a panel used to convert energy from the sun into electricity

specialize: to work at one specific job

starvation: the condition of not having enough food to eat

streetcar: a vehicle that runs on rails usually on city streets

submarine: a type of ship that can travel underwater

suburb: a neighborhood outside of a city

suffrage: the right to vote

surrender: to give up fighting

symbol: something that stands for something else

T

table of contents: a table that lists the chapters and other major sections of a book and the page numbers on which they start

technology: the practical use of new discoveries in science

temperate: neither too hot nor too cold

terrorist: a person who terrorizes, or frightens, people in order to get what he or she wants

textile mill: a mill for making cloth or clothes

theory: a possible explanation based on facts

threaten: to warn that something bad might happen

timeline: a line that shows when events in history happened in relation to one another

toleration: the act of allowing something to exist without fighting against it

toll: a fee

tourism: the industry that makes money from people who travel

trade: the business in which a person works

tradition: ways of celebrating culture that are passed down from one generation to the next generation

trauma: a serious injury

treason: the crime of plotting against or trying to overthrow the government

turning point: a specific time when an important change takes place

turnpike: a road drivers must pay to use

tutor: a person who instructs another

U

unconstitutional: goes against the principles in the constitution of the state or country

unemployed: having no job

unite: to come or join together

V

vaccine: a shot given to a person to prevent a disease

veteran: a person who has served in the military, especially a person who has fought in a war

veto: to reject

violent: marked by great force with the potential to cause property damage or injure people

volunteer: to work without being paid

W

wage: money a person earns for work he or she does, which is usually paid based on the number of hours worked

wampum: beads made from shells that Native Americans once used as money

wind turbine: a large windmill that converts the wind's energy into electricity

witness: to see something happen

Index

Credits

The following abbreviations are used for sources from which several images were obtained:

BC — Bettmann/Corbis
BSP — Big Stock Photos
GR — Gary Rasmussen
Granger — The Granger Collection, New York
HSM — Historic St. Mary's City
IRC — Instructional Resources Corporation: The History of Maryland Slide Collection
JB — Jon Burton
Jupiter — 2009 Jupiter Images Corporation
LOC — Library of Congress Prints and Photographs Division
MDHS — The Maryland Historical Society
MDA — The Maryland Archives
NARA — National Archives
NA — Neal Anderson
NWPA — North Wind Picture Archives
NYPL — New York Public Library
SS — Shutterstock.com

Cover: "The Inner Harbor of Baltimore—1983"
copyright © 2008 by Paul McGehee
paulmcgeheeart.com

Chapter 1: 2-3 Pete Hoffman/SS; 4 (t)Dino Ablakovic/SS, (l)spe/SS, (r) Tom Grundy/SS; 9 Ariel Skelley/Corbis; 12 BSP; 13 (t) Paul McGehee, (b) Filip Fuxa/SS; 16 (t) LOC, (b) BSP.

Chapter 2: 18-19 2265524729/SS; 20 Richard Thornton/SS; 21; 22 NASA; 30 Mary Terriberry/SS; 32 Glathrem/BSP; 33 (t) Blake Sell/Rueters/Corbis, (r) Bob Bianchard/SS, (b) Tdoes1/Dreamstime.com; 35 Baker, Will: Courtesy of the Chesapeake Bay Foundation; 36 (t) C. Kurt Holter/SS, (l) Alan Connell, (b) 4736202690/SS; 37 (t) Anton Albert/SS, (b) Paul A. Souders/Corbis; 38 Joshua Haviv/123RF; 39 (l) Keith Kiska/istockphoto.com, (b) niderlander/SS; 40 C. Kurt Holter/SS; 41 (l) digitalskillet/SS, (r) Suzanne Chapelle; 42 2265524729/SS; 43 (t) Tim Tadder/Corbis, (br) Monkey Business Photos/SS, (bl) Middleton Evans; 44 (t) Paul A. Souders/Corbis, (r) Robert Pernell/SS, (b) Nicolas Raymond/SS; 45 (l) Paul A. Souders/Corbis, (r) johannes compaan/SS; 46 Rob Marmion/SS; 47 GR; 48 iofoto/SS; 49 GR; 50 (l) U.S. Fish and Wildlife Services, DLS, (r) Paul A. Souders/Corbis; 51 LOC; 52 (tl) Anders Brownworth/SS, (tr) Albert Barr/SS, (bl) Lfink/SS, (br) Olga Bogatyrenko/SS.

Chapter 3: 54-55 David Wright Art; 56 Jon Burton; 57 NA; 59 LOC; 61 Elizabeth Kennedy Gische, 2008; 62 NWPA; 63 Pocumtuck Valley Memorial Association, Memorial Hall Museum, Deerfield, Massachusetts; 64 Martin Pate Art; 65 HSM; 66 Suzanne Chapelle; 67 (t) GR, (b) NWPA; 68 GR; 69 GR; 70 (l) Painting by Greg Harlin. Courtesy Frank H. McClug Museum, The University of Tennessee, Knoxville, (r) HSM; 71 GR; 72 GR; 73 GR; 74 Julie Knight; 75 (l) LOC, (r) NA; 76 HSM.

Chapter 4: 78-79 Colonial Williamsburg; 80 LOC; 82 NWPA; 83 (t) LOC, (b) Sidney E. King/NPS/Colonial National Historical Park; 84 (t) Ed Young/Corbis, (b) BC; 85 LOC; 86 MDHS; 87 LOC; 88 NWPA; 89 Granger; 90 MDHS; 91 (t) MDA, (b) LOC; 92 IRC; 93 HSM; 94 ; John Vehar; 96 (l) LOC, (r) NWPA; 97 GR; 98 NWPA; 99 NWPA; 100 Sidney E. King/NPS/Colonial National Historical Park; 101 Granger; 102 Sidney E. King/NPS/Colonial National Historical Park; 103 Granger; 104 BC; 105 NWPA; 106 (l) NWPA, (r) NA; 107 MDHS; 108 MDHS; 109 MDHS; 110 BC; 111 Sidney E. King/NPS/Colonial National Historical Park; 112 MDHS; 113 BC; 114 HSM.

Chapter 5: 116-117 Kemmelmeyer Frederick/Bridgeman Art Library; 119 SuperStock, inc; 120 (l) ; 121 NWPA; 122 NWPA; 123 Francis Blackwell Mayer; 124 (t) LOC, (b) MDHS; 125 NWPA; 126 NWPA; 128 LOC; 129 Richard T. Nowitz/Corbis; 130 NARA; 131 (l) MDHS, (cl) MDHS, (cr) MDA, (r) IRC; 132 (t) NWPA, (b) LOC; 133 (r) MDHS, (l) Granger; 134 (t) LOC, (b) Sidney E. King/NPS/Colonial National Historical Park; 135 C Inger/Corbis; 136 John Trumbull/Bridgeman; 137 (t) IRC, (b) MDA; 138 NARA; 139 (l) Hy Hintermeister/SuperStock, Inc., (r) Granger; 140 MDHS.

Chapter 6: 142-143 MDHS; 144 MDHS; 145 (t) LOC, (b) MDHS; 146 (t) IRC, (b) NWPA; 147 (t) Star- Spangled Banner Flag House, (b) LOC; 148 Granger; 149 NWPA; 150 MDHS; 152 LOC; 153 JB; 154 BC; 156 (l) IRC, r) NWPA; 158 BC; 159 LOC; 160 C&O Cannal Museum; 161 IRC; 162 Enoch Pratt Free Library; 163 Bridgeman Art Library; 164 Granger; 165 (t) MDA, (bl) LOC, (br) LOC; 166 LOC.

Chapter 7: 168-169 LOC; 171 LOC; 172 NWPA; 173 Granger; 174 LOC; 175 LOC; 176 NWPA; 177 NWPA; 178 LOC; 179 (t) John Davies/SuperStock, Inc, (c) LOC, (b) NYPL; 179 LOC; 182 Enoch Pratt Free Library; 183 LOC; 184 NWPA; 186 LOC; 187 (t) Granger, (b) LOC; 189 LOC; 190 National Park Service; 191 LOC; 192 LOC; 193 LOC; 194 LOC; 196 Appomattox Court House National Park Service; 197 LOC; 198 Corbis; 199 LOC; 201 LOC.

Chapter 8: 202-203 LOC; 204-205 LOC; 206 LOC; 208 LOC; 209 (t) LOC, (b) MDHS; 210 LOC; 211 LOC; 212 LOC; 213 LOC; 214 LOC; 215 (t) Morgan Lane Photography/SS, (b) LOC; 216 LOC; 217 (c) JB, (r) MDHS; 218 LOC; 219 MDA; 220 LOC; 221 BC; 222 Enoch Pratt Free Library; 223 Richard Thrunton/SS; 224 LOC.

Chapter 9: 226-227 LOC; 228 LOC; 229 LOC; 230 LOC; 231 LOC; 232 (l) Christophe Testi/Shutterstock, (r) LOC; 233 LOC; 234 LOC; 235 LOC; 236 BC; 237 (l) LOC, (r) Suzanne Chapelle; 238 (t) BC, (b) LOC; 239 (t) LOC, (b) IRC; 241 LOC; 242 (t) MDHS; 243 LOC; 244 LOC; 245 LOC; 246 LOC; 247 LOC; 249 MDA.

Chapter 10: 250-251 Kevin Fleming/Corbis; 252 BC; 253 H. Armstrong Roberts/Corbis; 254 Ray Cornia; 255 (t) Paul A. Souders/Corbis, (b) Superstock; 256 LOC; 257 (t) LOC, (b) Graham De'ath/SS; 258 BC; 259 LOC; 260 BC; 261 LOC; 262 (l) LOC, (r) BC; 263 BC; 264 LOC; 265 BC; 266 Owen Franken/Corbis; 267 (t) Middleton Evans, (b) Alan Mason Cheney Medical Archives, Johns Hopkins Medical Institutions; 268 (t) Roger Ressmeyer/Corbis, (b) NASA; 269 NASA; 270 Suzanne Chapelle; 271 Corbis/Superstock; 272 Suzanne Chapelle; 273 Suzanne Chapelle; 274 Galina Barskaya/SS; 275 Paul A. Souders/Corbis; 276 Gelpi/SS; 278 (t) Sean Adair/Rueters/Corbis, (b) Rueters/Corbis; 279 US Army; 280 LOC.

Chapter 11: 282-283 Paul A. Souders/Corbis; 284 Olga Bogatyrenko/SS; 285 NARA; 286-287 JB; 290-291 Jupiter Images; 292 Gail Burton/AP Images; 295 Mike O'Dell/Office of the Governor; 296 Samuel Colbert/AC/MDCOURT; 297 capturefoto/SS; 298 MDA; 300 Paul A. Souders/Corbis; 301 Anne Arundel County; 303 Jim Parkin/SS; 304 Rob Marmiom/SS; 306 Lisa F. Young/SS; 307 Leland Bobbe/Corbis; 308 Suzanne Chapelle; 309 Lisa F. Young/SS.

Chapter 12: 312-313 Paul A. Souders/Corbis; 314 GeoM/SS; 315 Paul A. Souders/Corbis; 316 Images by Yancy/SS; 318 (t) SS, (b) Corbis; 319 (t) US Mint, (b) Tom Oliveira/SS; 320 (t) steve estvanik/SS, (b) Bryce Newell/SS; 321 Louie Psihoyos/Corbis; 322 (l) Lorelyn Medina/SS, (c) Rick Lord/SS, (r) iStockphoto.com; 323 Melissa King/SS; 325 Denisenko/SS; 327 NA; 328 NWPA; 329 Luca Flor/SS; 330 BP Solar Industries; 332 (t) tdoes/Big Stock Photo, (b) Kevin Fleming/Corbis; 333 (t) 2265524729/SS, (b) Kevin Burke/Corbis; 334 (l) Peter Howard, (r) Andrews Airforce Base/US Airforce; 335 Steve Ruark/Baltimore Special Olympics; 336 Suzanne Chapelle; 337 Suzanne Chapelle; 339 copyright 2009 Andy Singer/Cagle Cartoons.

All other images are from Gibbs Smith, Publisher Archives; Photos.com; or Clipart.